WIELOPOLE/WIELOPOLE

WIELOPOLE/WIELOPOLE

An exercise in theatre

TADEUSZ KANTOR

Translated from the Polish

by Mariusz Tchorek

and G.M. Hyde

With an introduction by

G.M. Hyde

Marion Boyars

London · New York

Published in Great Britain and the United States in 1990
by Marion Boyars Publishers
24 Lacy Road, London SW15 1NL and
26 East 33rd Street, New York, NY 10016

Distributed in the United States and Canada by
Rizzoli International Publications, New York

Distributed in Australia by
Wild and Woolley, Glebe, N.S.W.

British Library Cataloguing in Publication Data

Kantor, Tadeusz, 1915–
   Wielopole/Wielopole: an exercise in
   theatre.
   I. Title
   891.8′527

Library of Congress Catologing in Publication Data

Kantor, Tadeusz, 1915–
   Wielopole/Wielopole.
   Translation of Wielopole, Wielopole.
   I. Title
PG7170.A54W5413   1988   891.8′525   88–14163

ISBN 0-7145-2782-3 Original paperback edition.

Photographs by Maurizio Buscarino
by Permission of Ubulibri, Florence

CONTENTS

The publishers wish to thank the
European Community Commission
whose generous support made the
publication of this book possible.

The publishers also wish to
thank Adam Czerniawski
for his editorial assistance.

INTRODUCTION

A new lease of death:

Tadeusz Kantor and *Wielopole/Wielopole*

G.M. Hyde

Tadeusz Kantor's reputation in Britain has been somewhat overshadowed by that of other Polish directors, despite the considerable acclaim won by *Dead Class* at the Edinburgh Festival in 1976. In France, Germany, and the United States, as well as in Italy where his *Cricot 2* company was based for some years, the situation is different, as it is in his native Poland, where he has been hailed as the foremost living director and has even (after decades of neglect) won the approval of the press and the more 'official' representatives of the media. But although fame has come late, Kantor is by no means a newcomer to the arts scene, and has been working as a painter since before the Second World War. In this introduction I want to provide a sketch, necessarily incomplete, of his development as an artist, and try to situate him in relation to the mainstream of European avant-gardes, as well as offering my own interpretation of what his Polishness means. Both of these emphases are equally necessary, since *Wielopole/Wielopole* is from one poil ι of view deeply rooted in a specific time and place, the Polish Galicia of Kantor's childhood which has changed profoundly yet stayed strangely the same; while from another standpoint it is as rootless, or as rooted in the void, as the Dada from which ultimately it springs.

The 'rootedness' of *Wielopole/Wielopole*, however, has nothing to do with nostalgia. The title of the play contains a characteristic *reduplication* of the name of the small town where Kantor was born (on 16 April 1915), reminding us of the *pastness* of the past as much as of its presence. To remember a place, a person, an event, is to construct a special kind of *space* in which an encounter between past and present becomes possible. Memory, far from merging past and present, works to create differences, disjunctions, it sharpens the sense of loss which situates us, too, among the dead. This mirror-effect of the title is echoed throughout the text of the play, as well as in the way that (in this volume taken as a whole) scenes are reworked in rehearsal notes or in theoretical texts. There is, moreover, a conscious 'doubling' of actors, or of actors with inanimate mannequins. The Priest is the most significant, belonging as he does to this world and the next; but there is also the comic double act of the twin uncles, where a mirror is held up not to the 'real' world but to another mirror, and another, *ad infinitum*. There are re-runs of entire episodes in the play and the notes to the play (and in the very first scene, the two uncles keep crossing vertiginously over the barrier between represented space and real space, 'setting the scene' like stagehands but from within the fictional world of the play). All of this points to the larger issues of representation, imitation, copying that constitute the substance of Kantor's metaphysical obsession with realism. Kantor objects with an almost Platonic fervour to the art that is no more than the form of a form, the shadow of a shadow. Like other reformers of the stage, Kantor is opposed to illusionism, but the terms of his opposition, derived partly from Polish sources (especially the ideas of Witkiewicz), are, as we shall see, highly idiosyncratic.

Kantor came to the theatre from the fine arts rather than from literature, a fact which is everywhere apparent in his work. He finished his studies (painting and theatrical design) in Krakow on the eve of the last war. There is no need to recapitulate here the cataclysmic impact of the Second World War on Poland and its people, especially the Jewish population. That Kantor should have survived it is a kind of miracle: but when he recalls the war, as he does in this volume, it is characteristically in terms of a significant *artistic* event, the painful return of Odysseus from another, more remote, war, in Wyspiański's play *The Return of Odysseus*. Kantor produced this play in the Underground Theatre in Krakow in 1944, and attaches such importance to it not just because it was virtually his début as a director, but also because it contains the germ of all his thinking about the theatre. Homer's wanderer, on loan to Wyspiański, reduplicated by Kantor (who deals very freely with dramatic texts), entering the play as a shell-shocked soldier who has wandered in from the street, is the type of the actor in the degraded spectacle of Kantor's later Theatre of Death, on loan from some shady employment exchange, a refugee from the void. Entering the bomb-damaged room he sits and stares, traumatized, into the distance. At length, turning to the audience (who share his space, since the room is also the auditorium) he pronounces Wyspiański's words, which are no longer Wyspiański's: 'I am Ulysses, come back from Troy.' Like Joyce's Bloom, this Ulysses is Everyman, but a traumatized Everyman from the boundaries of life and death, a ghastly figure who bears little resemblance to Joyce's *homme moyen sensuel*. Behind him stretches a void, a frozen unspoken world, the world of the *text* which is also the world of *the dead* (characterized by fixed relations, determined chains of event and of causality, a totalizing *structure* where nothing can be out of place). A theatrical performance is, for Kantor, not a realization of the text but (to borrow his own term) a 'text-mincer' that cuts across or runs parallel to (but separate from) the world of the text (the world of the dead). Yet as he says in his *Theatre of Death* manifesto, the living *need* the dead, because

> It is only the dead who become
> *perceptible* (for the living)
> thus winning, for this highest price,
> their separate status
> distinction
> their SHAPE
> garish
> and almost
> *clownish*.

It is tempting to see Kantor's preoccupation with the world of the dead as a distinctively Polish trait, though if we do, we must at the same time recognize that he would be quick to dissociate himself from Polish messianism. Romantic literature, from Mickiewicz's *Dziady (Forefathers' Eve)* to Wyspiański's *Wesele (The Wedding)*, takes a portentous, apocalyptic, mystical view of the communings of spirits and demiurges with the world of the living. Daemonic presences embody the repressed, subterranean aspirations of Poland's divided self in these and other Romantic works: while in Kantor's theatre the daemonic presence is that of Kantor himself, in evening dress, tieless, moving unseen among his actors. Ancestor worship in Polish literature is directly connected with martyrology, the respect paid to those who fell in the struggle for nationhood, and with such sentiments Kantor has little to do; yet it is hard to imagine his grotesque deaths and resurrections in *Wielopole/Wielopole* without the Polish 'Zaduszki', or All Souls' Eve, where the dead commune with the living. Kantor's Polishness, here as elsewhere, reveals itself through his scepticism and sense of the absurd as much as through his fascination with ritual and fantasy. In this respect we may see *Wielopole/Wielopole* (in an image used by Kantor himself in his *Maly Manifest* of 1978) as a return of the prodigal: but it is a prodigal who has no intention of renouncing his hard-won ironic detachment. His sensibility was formed by the European avant-garde: to trace the stages of his development is to pass through many of the major movements in contemporary painting. After absorbing the work of Polish avant-gardists (Chwistek, Czyżewski, Strzemiński, and Kobro), and in particular the Constructivism that played a major part in Eastern European theatre, Kantor was deeply influenced by Dada, drawing inspiration from it for his subsequent environmental art, happenings, ready-mades, and ventures into conceptualism. Dada provided, and continues to provide, a state of what Kantor calls *fluidity*, and what he refers to as 'the provocative presence of the object', an important component in his brand of realism. For Kantor, the Dada object has proved more permanently disturbing than the dream image of Surrealism. The afterlife of junk, wreckage (*'wrak'*) is another manifestation of death: things become themselves somewhere between the scrapheap and infinity.

There is, says Kantor, no history of twentieth-century art other than the history of the avant-garde. Nevertheless, his *direct* experience of contemporary French art came relatively late, in Krakow in 1946 with the exhibition of French painting. In the following year he visited Paris; but characteristically observes that he was as much impressed by the Palais de la Découverte as by the Louvre. This 'ant-hill' of 'density' (*'zagfęszczenie'* is a favourite term of approval) with its non-anthropocentric view of Nature echoed his own creative preoccupations. Here, no doubt, originated the fiendish contrivances (annihilation machines built of piles of chairs, birth-and-death machines) that play a major part in his later work and in his theory of the 'bio-object'. But it may well be the case that the fascination of the Palais de la Découverte also explains why Constructivism could not ultimately provide Kantor with the model of a non-representational theatre. To experience the archaeology of inventions is to experience their pathos. Kantor denies that he has any interest in the 'poetry of the scrap-heap', which is just another kind of sentimentality, and there is no reason to doubt this. Nevertheless, the interest of machines and of objects for him certainly resides in the way they participate in and express the organic: it has very little to do with the utopian order and geometry of Constructivism. Kantor's own paintings of the 1940s (entitled 'metaphysical' paintings) are a fusion of Cubist and Surrealist elements, but with his emphasis on elements of stress and of tension in the pictorial space (sometimes suggesting Futurism), and in what he called 'umbrella' space — expanding and contracting in different directions simultaneously — we become aware of a dramatic, even theatrical, element. When traditional perspective is abandoned, he says, such lines of stress (in a multiple construction of space) take its place. If this is an echo of Futurism, it is a Futurism with a strongly experiential, even existential, dimension.

The transition between Kantor's paintings and the founding of the *Cricot 2* theatre in 1956 can be accounted for in terms of his involvement with another movement in (French) painting, the so-called *art informel* of Fautrier, Dubuffet, Michaux, Riopelle, Matthieu and others (the term itself was devised by the critic Michel Tapié in 1950). Like Tachisme, *art informel* breaks with geometrical abstraction of all kinds and considers painting rather in terms of 'exploding outwards' (Kantor's own term). The imagination is always in a state of *stress*, the *process* is the work, there is no absolute division between creativity (*twórczość*) and work (*sztuka*). There ought then to be a natural affinity between *art informel* and theatre, and indeed Kantor felt able to appropriate the term *informel* for one period of his own work. When Witkiewicz's *The Cuttlefish* was mounted by the newly formed *Cricot 2* company in 1956, the programme cover was an *informel* painting by Kantor. *Informel* relations of stress and tension between the different components of the spectacle permeated the production: in addition to a deliberate lack of congruence between text and performance, the actors were set at odds with their roles. Improvisation has never been a major part of Kantor's theatre, but even at this point in time the actor's relation to puppet and mannequin was emphasized above their relation to 'living', or verisimilar, 'characters'.

There was, in other words, no question here, or in Kantor's other Witkiewicz productions (*The Little Manor* 1961, *The Madman and the Nun* 1963, *The Water Hen* 1967, *The Shoemakers* 1972, *Lovelies and Dowdies* 1973) of transposing the plays on to the stage. An eccentric genius, Witkiewicz easily becomes 'stupid farce' (Kantor's own phrase) if the *literary* intricacies of his texts are simply translated into action. By isolating key images, motifs, gestures, and counterpointing them with textual elements (themselves considered simply as part of the raw semantic material) the production takes shape in terms of the given theatrical space, movement, gesture. The question of the nature and identity of the theatrical space has of course preoccupied directors and theoreticians of the theatre since Edward Gordon Craig (an innovator to whom Kantor makes frequent reference). For Kantor, however, the much-vaunted removal of the invisible wall between stage and audience is a non-event contrived by the pseudo avant-garde (including Grotowski). Useless to pretend, he thinks, that the actor moves on the same plane as the spectator: the actor is caught in the world of the dead, he is not free, as we are, to leave the theatre, and we are always aware of this radical difference; never more so, in fact, than when we are thrust into the midst of the action, as we are by those directors who insist on acting out the play *around* the audience (for Kantor this kind of 'total theatre' is simply the nadir of naturalism.)

On the other hand, the theatrical space and the objects which populate it cannot simply be left to their own devices. 'Props' and costumes cannot be thought of merely as decorative elements. Kantor's solution is to situate his objects on a borderline between functionalism and self-sufficiency. At this point of tension between the 'real' and the 'represented' worlds objects become most completely themselves (between, as Kantor puts it, the scrap-heap and infinity). This is the point he is making about the wardrobe, much more than a prop but much less abstract than a symbol. The culmination of Kantor's thinking about theatrical illusion up to now is his so-called Theatre of Death (including *Dead Class* (1975), *Wielopole/Wielopole* (1981), and *Où Sont les Neiges d'Antan* (1984)). In his manifesto of the Theatre of Death Kantor harks back to Craig's well-known critique of the actor in the name of the 'Übermarionette'. It seemed to Craig that the actor posed the greatest threat to the theatre, because he introduced into an otherwise homogeneous and controlled world a set of variables, an arbitrary human element. Craig's answer to this was that the actor should give way to the puppet: by returning to some kind of marionette-play, the dramatist and director could free themselves from psychology. Kantor's answer is different: the puppet is not so much the *alternative* to psychological realism as (if we think historically) the objectification of the repressed part of the psyche. From the late eighteenth century onward, the fascination with the homunculus and mechanical men, the automaton, represents the dark side of the enlightenment, the rational man's fear of the world of the dead (by which he is also fascinated). This world we carry inside us, like a time-bomb, and our lives are lived according to its 'text', its hidden imperatives. It is, in Kantor's view, the unconscious as well. Our only chance of encountering this unknown world face to face is through theatre, where the actor/marionette can act out the inner contradictions of our dual allegiance to the living and the dead. The actor is thus another kind of *emballage* (*ambalaż*), the 'wrapped' object that is most completely itself by virtue of its loss of identity. What we notice in *Dead Class* and after is a deepening subjectivity, represented through the way the living actor enters directly into contact with the anti-self of the dead world (like the Priest who plays a major role in *Wielopole/Wielopole*). The confusion of living and dead can equally be comic-grotesque, or Kafkaesque (for once the adjective is merited), where we enter an 'automatized' world of compulsive, traumatized ritual, full of nightmarish running on the spot, of vague, frightened responses to indeterminate threats. Belated inheritors of the Romantic double, Kantor's waxwork dummies make no claim to come from any transcendental realm, but embody a 'lower order' reality. The theatre of death is full of personages and objects 'from the margins' of reality, the discarded debris of people and things (like the school benches in *Dead Class* where characters rehearse the petty humiliations and squabbles of their childhood). In *Wielopole/Wielopole* we are not to imagine that we are 'really' watching the members of Kantor's family re-enacting the return of the Father, the death of the Priest, the marriage of Marian and Helena: far from it. The 'characters' we watch are all, Kantor suggests, hired from an agency, doubling in other low-life roles while offering (for a fee) to enact the eternal verities of family life. This collection of part-time con-men, ponces, and whores, assigned the 'sacred' roles of father, uncle, priest, aunt, play out the 'family romance' without conviction. In *Dead Class* the characters are a compendium of 'marginal' types drawn from three (in particular) Polish writers of genius who constitute a kind of modernist pantheon, Witkiewicz, Schulz, and Gombrowicz (Kantor now deservedly takes his place alongside them). The core idea of *Dead Class*, where adults return to the schoolroom and rediscover their capacity for futile vindictiveness, aggression, competitiveness, owes much to Gombrowicz's absurdist first novel *Ferdydurke*, with its bitter celebration of humanity's eternal attachment to its own immaturity, intensified in the face of an ignorant and obscurantist authority that tries to turn everyone into an eternal schoolboy. Here again, one might find specific allusion to the 'Polish condition', but again it is refracted through a prism of scepticism and irony. Here is the 'marginality' of which Kantor says that it is central to the real experience of the modern world, where truth has retreated to the boundary. Schulz, for example, writes from within a world where not to be of the centre is the only tenable kind of centrality. His tales of provincial inertia and paralysis are at the same time celebrations of the power of the imagination: they confirm Walter Benjamin's thesis that 'Boredom is the dream bird that hatches the egg of experience.' The life of Schulz's characters (if they may be called characters) is lived somewhere between the Baudelairean extremes of ennui, spleen, and ideal. It is as if modernist literature had found a local habitation and a name among the Jewish and Judaeo-Christian communities of Polish Galicia. The alienation of the great poet of the city has become the marginality of a whole community. We in the West keep moving on, or maybe delude ourselves that we can. In the world of Schulz's stories, there is nowhere to go. Who is to say that Schulz's paranoia is a less truthful version of the human condition than the American dream?

Which brings us back to *Wielopole/Wielopole*, the most personal of Kantor's works, in which he deliberately paces out the boundaries of his own psyche, intervening from time to time *in propria persona* (as of course he does in other productions) like the god in the machine. The play opens with him introducing (silently) the members of his family, 'imprinted' ectoplasmally on the room that is to serve as the claustrophobic model of all time and space. The uncles (doubles) act out their infantile game of recognizing and rejecting the 'world' they are constructing, with a clownish obsessiveness. Kantor in fact constantly refers to his play as a 'show' (a word I use in English with misgivings), and compares it to an entertainment in the Big Top, aligning it (in Dada style) with the world of the mountebank rather than the world of the tragedian. This neurotic and obsessive behaviour of the uncles is interrupted (a recurrent pattern) by an intruder, in this case Uncle Staś, the Siberian deportee. He might be seen as a 'historical' presence in the family scenario, reminding us of the fate of thousands of Poles and a degraded echo of Poland's 'Romantic' struggle for selfhood (his phoney violin plays Chopin). The Uncles treat him (and everything else) as an inanimate 'prop' to help them to set the scene (from which, it subsequently turns out, they were in any case absent), and to introduce the other members of the family, grouped around the dying priest and squabbling about the will. Death enters in person, in the 'lower order' guise of the widow of the local photographer (photography both *records* the ceremonial moments of life and annihilates them; the photographer brings events closer, but freezes them by distancing us from the dead image of what once was living). The Priest, appropriately, is chosen to enact in the most concrete form this life/death ambivalence, materialized in the shape of his interchangeability with his own waxwork effigy, turning on the axis of a massive two-faced bed-machine, rotated by a crankshaft.

Distant and distorted echoes of Poland's history of military struggle and insurrection enter in the guise of the platoon: significantly they occupy the same *space* as the family (when Kantor sets his plays in *real* spaces he achieves precisely this effect of *density*). By a sinister and absurd association of ideas, the camera becomes a machine gun, spreading 'literal' death and destruction, and we are back with the marriage of Kantor's parents, a ritual traumatized from the outset by the shock of death and separation. In such obscure ways are personal and public histories interwoven in an erratic cycle of death and resurrection.

To take the reader step by step through Kantor's text would of course constitute a fatal betrayal of his purpose. The words on the page are, as I have said, only one element of the whole (the photographs in this volume go some way towards providing another). Moreover, rehearsal notes and theoretical pieces keep constructing new perspectives on the action, in such a way that a definitive version is indefinitely postponed. The point is to be ready to respond to Kantor's startling imaginative shifts. When, for instance, he constructs a provisional equation between the platoon and the audience, inviting us to contemplate our own anonymity and expropriation in the guise of their uniformity and helplessness, and then suggests that they stand for our suppressed knowledge of our own death, and thus constitute the quintessential statement of the role of the actor, Kantor's lateral thinking may be hard to follow: yet all of this constitutes a consistent position, arrived at over many years, and is far from being a display of legerdemain.

I have tried to resist the temptation to comment on Kantor's view of what Freud called the 'family romance' from a psychoanalytical standpoint. Like everything else in the play, it is compounded of clowning, horror, farce, and pathos. The ironic parallels that Kantor constructs with the Holy Family and the Last Supper are in some danger of appearing contrived to an English reader, but the element of the grotesque and the blasphemous in representing the sacred is a deep and vital presence in Polish (Catholic) culture. What must be very striking for an English reader is surely

Kantor's refusal to psychoanalyse his sacred and profane families. The reasons for this are doubtless connected with the relatively low profile of Freudian psychology in present-day Poland, but in addition it should by now be clear to the reader that Kantor's art is *against interpretation*: to rationalize the irrational is no part of his purpose. Kantor's absurdist view of the world is posited upon randomness, chaos, fragmentariness; he would not be able to work with 'totalizing' philosophies like Freudianism or Marxism. The texts in this volume do not constitute a finished work: the work (*sztuka*) cannot be finished because the creative impulse (*twórczość*) continues to play upon it. Not for nothing did Kantor take *Wielopole/Wielopole* back to Wielopole, to perform it in the church in his native town. The report of this event in *Polityka* catches the note of random repeatability: The Room (says the article), the childhood room where it all began, was constructed as a set in front of the altar: but it looked (despite this 'sacred' space) 'like rooms that had existed — that still exist — within walking distance' of that very church.

Kantor's playscript may strike the reader as sketchy, even awkward. It should be borne in mind that it is only the bare bones of the spectacle, fleshed out in performance with rich visual effects. In addition, it is intrinsic to Kantor's absurdism that language should keep missing its target, so that the characters talk at cross-purposes and at tangents. The misunderstandings that ensue contribute to the effect of 'density'. The text is an object, a log-book or palimpsest of the traces left by a series of performances, or 'happenings'.

CHARACTERS

Uncle Karol
Uncle Olek
Auntie Mánka
Auntie Józka
Priest/Granpa/Great Uncle
Grandma
Uncle Stasio/Deportee
Photographer/Widow
Mother Helka
Father
Adaś
Soldiers — a platoon of conscripts

WIELOPOLE/WIELOPOLE

The Play

ACT ONE

THE WEDDING

Scene 1

MYSELF

Sitting in the centre of the stage. The text of my part, as follows, must remain unspoken.

Here is my Grandmother, my mother's mother, Katarzyna.
And that's her brother, the Priest.
Some used to call him uncle.
He will die shortly.
My father sits over there.
The first from the left.
On the reverse of this photograph he sends his greetings.
Date: 12th September 1914.
Mother Helka will be here any minute.
The rest are Uncles and Aunts.
They went the way of all flesh, somewhere in the world.
Now they are in the room, imprinted as memories:
Uncle Karol, Uncle Olek, Auntie Mańka, Auntie Józka.
From this moment on, their fortunes begin to change passing through a series of radical alterations,
often quite embarrassing, such as they would have been unable to face, had they been among the living.

Scene 2

The room of my childhood. I keep setting it up; it keeps dying.

UNCLE KAROL

He looks round the room. Recognizing the place, he grins at himself and his memories. Something is out of order, though: his attention is caught by a black suitcase.

**A suitcase . . .
The suitcase was on the table.
Correct!**

He comes forward to the table, touches the suitcase, just to be certain. The suitcase brings back a memory. He sees Uncle Olek sitting motionless in a chair.

**Uncle Olek!
Surely, Uncle Olek wasn't
sitting down, was he?
He was standing, or walking
. . .**

UNCLE OLEK

Standing up. He, too, examines the suitcase intently.

**The suitcase was on the
wardrobe . . .**

He carries the suitcase over with great care. On the way he bumps into a chair.

What about that chair?

UNCLE KAROL

Grandpa? Is it?

Noticing Grandpa-Priest's body. The dead Priest sits in a rickety chair.

**But Grandpa wasn't sitting
down either.
Or standing up!**

Quite astounded at his discovery. Each Uncle remains wrapped in his memories and meditations.
Doggedly.

UNCLE OLEK

**What about the chair, then?
The one next to the table?**

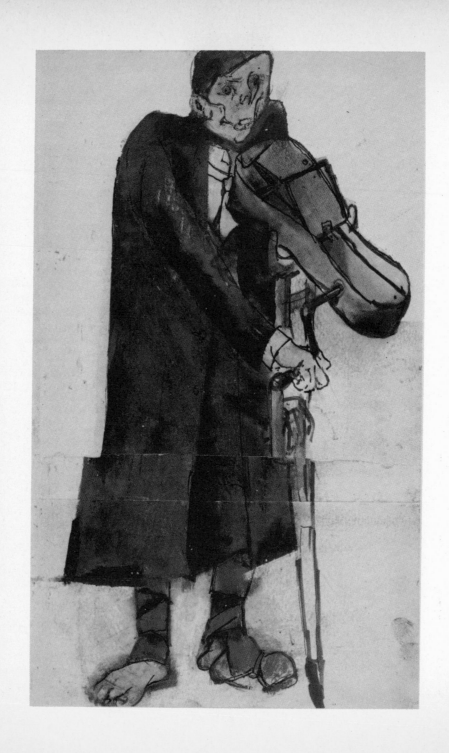

And where's the table?
There was one in front of the
chair.
Next to it, I say.
And what about the door?

UNCLE KAROL

He lifts the Priest's body from the chair.
Something continually escapes him.
Now he remembers.

Grandpa was not sitting!
He was lying down!
Sure he was.
His head at the bedhead.

He lays the Priest on the bed.

Now, the door was opposite the
window.

UNCLE OLEK

Trying hard to be systematic.

The window close to the table . . .
The wardrobe in the corner . . .
But what about the table?
Was the table there at all?

He is besieged by doubts.

UNCLE KAROL

When Uncle was opening the
door to come in,
the window was opposite the
door!

He stares at the door, which is opening at this
very moment. Somebody is pushing it slowly
from outside.

DEPORTEE

Enter Uncle Stasio, a Siberian deportee and
a busker rolled into one. A down-and-out in
tattered army uniform. He holds a violin
case. He staggers through the door. His face
is haggard. A walking corpse. He peers into
the room he left long ago: he hasn't the
courage to walk in. So exhausted is he that he
must lean against the doorframe. His
busker's hand reaches out for a concealed
handle and the melody of a carol emerges
haltingly from the violin case. He lays the
battered violin case carefully on the floor:
then he falls down.

UNCLE KAROL

Stepping up to him, he twists Uncle Stasio's
head to examine it. He has recognized him.

Uncle Staś

Back home.
Olek!
Staś is back!

UNCLE OLEK

He approaches the Deportee. They both lift him carefully and prop him up against the doorframe like a marionette, the way you might lay out a corpse in a coffin. They walk off, whispering to each other.

UNCLE KAROL   **It's Staś.**
He's back.
UNCLE OLEK   **He's got lice.**
UNCLE KAROL   **What a disgrace!**
UNCLE OLEK   **What shall we do?**

Both ponder.

UNCLE KAROL   **Just say we don't know him;**
there are lots like him
nowadays.

He closes the door after the retreating Deportee. They both try to blot out the embarrassing incident.

UNCLE KAROL   **When Uncle Karol was closing**
the door,
that window was opposite the
door.
UNCLE OLEK   **If the suitcase was on the**
wardrobe,
the chair was next to the
table,
the window shut,
then was Uncle Olek here?
Right, Józka was lying down . . .
No, there was no chair!
But what about the table?

He drags the table to the door, ignoring the sprawling bodies of Auntie Józka and Grandma.
Deep in thought.

UNCLE KAROL
Grandma stood next to
Grandpa.
Grandpa was lying down.
Still, Józka was not there!

UNCLE OLEK

He struggles to hold the table over Auntie Józka's head.

And the table wasn't here, either!
Grandpa was in here, true, but Józka wasn't.

UNCLE KAROL

Agreeing with him.

Right, she wasn't.
Auntie Józka was missing.

Uncle Olek puts the table down.
Together they carry Auntie Józka's body out.

Auntie Mańka wasn't sitting here.
She was absent too.

Carrying out Auntie Mańka.
Doggedly trying to come to grips with the problem of the table.

UNCLE OLEK

What about this table, then?

Pulling the table up to the door.

This one.
The table right here . . .

In the end he manages to carry it out.

UNCLE KAROL

The door opposite the window.
Grandpa in bed, his head at the bedhead.

UNCLE OLEK

Recoiling under the pressure of his memories.

But what about Grandma?

UNCLE KAROL

Both feel rushed. Everything gets jumbled up.

And the wardrobe!
Where was the wardrobe?

UNCLE OLEK

Hardly able to keep pace, he tries his best to be precise.

The door opposite the window.
As he was opening the door,
he could see the window and the table.

UNCLE KAROL

Hurriedly enumerating.

The table, the window,
the wardrobe next to it.

It dawns upon him.

Grandma!
Grandma was standing up!

UNCLE OLEK	**Grandpa was lying down.**	
UNCLE KAROL		Taking stock.
	Grandma was standing, the door was opposite the window, the table was not here. Grandma next to Grandpa. She was standing.	
		They lift Grandma from the ground.
UNCLE OLEK	**Uncle Karol . . . was he there? No, he wasn't! Neither was I! But the chair was. The door, the window, Uncle Karol . . . What about Karol? Was Karol there? I wasn't there.**	
UNCLE KAROL	**Was I there? No, I wasn't. I wasn't there either. Olek was not there, neither was I.**	
UNCLE OLEK	**I was not here.**	
UNCLE KAROL	**Neither was I.**	
UNCLE OLEK	**Karol!**	
UNCLE KAROL	**Olek!**	
		Going out.
UNCLE OLEK	**Karol!**	
UNCLE KAROL	**Olek!**	
UNCLE OLEK	**Karol!**	
UNCLE KAROL	**Olek!**	
		Both vanish. The stage is empty.

Scene 3

On the bed of sickness.

Scene 4

The last rites.

GRANDMA   Sings Psalm CX at the bed of the dying Priest.

**The Lord said
unto my Lord,
Sit thou at my right
hand,
until I
make thine enemies
thy footstool.**

While intoning the Psalm, she inserts a metal
bed-pan under his body. She does not
interrupt her singing. A large chorus of men
and women from a Carpathian village join in
with her. The door opens. In the hall the
dead body of a woman in a wedding gown can
be seen. In the gap of the doorway a bizarre
rattling tin camera appears. The
Photographer (female) is there, too, but she
is not allowed in, because Grandma stops
her. She yells:

**Not yet!
Not yet!**

The Priest shows signs of life still.
Grandma repeats her Psalm as well as her
operation with the bed-pan. The door opens,
but Grandma once again steps in to prevent
the Photographer intruding.

**Not yet!
Not yet!**

Another round of the same actions and the Psalm. Apparently the Priest has given up the ghost, for the Photographer manages to make her way into the room, squeezing the camera in with her. Grandma pauses stock-still like Niobe over the death bed, with the bed-pan in her clasped hands.

Scene 5

The local photographer's visit, not the one to end all visits, but effective as ever.

PHOTOGRAPHER

The widow of the owner of the local photographic studio (known as 'Ricordo') and a foul skivvy, from the parish charnel house, rolled into one. A dismal agent of death. Bluntly thrusting in her hooded hand-cart with a built-in camera. She behaves in a careless, slapdash fashion, showing the typical callousness of her trade. The ebb and flow of the Psalm continues. Having pulled her cart up in the middle of the room, the sullen photographer expels Grandma and slowly closes the door behind her. She now remains tête-a-tête with her model and prey. For a moment she pauses to contemplate the scene, as befits her discreet profession.

Scene 6

The local photographer alone with her model. The mechanics of death and his secret agent.

Closing the door after Grandma, she lays her hand on the doorknob as though on a tombstone. She checks her camera, in a slapdash fashion, then makes for the bed. Only now is she ready to perform her proper duties, her sullen rite.

The bed is a piece of machinery, a revolving machine of death. The top, made of unplaned boards, can rotate around a shaft, which ends in cog-wheels and a crank. As the top is made to rotate, each of its sides becomes alternately the upper or the under side. For the time being we can see the priest lying on top, a barefoot wax figure in a mortuary gown.

The Photographer carefully wipes the mechanism of the bed with a wet rag. The volume of the Psalm increases. She begins to turn the crank with the unction due to a *Requiem*. As the bed gradually turns round, the dead Priest, the one in the coarse mortuary gown, disappears. The same Priest (an actor) emerges from underneath. This time he is ceremonially vested: a glistening cassock, a biretta and patent-leather shoes as for the coffin. The hands folded. The Photographer swiftly props the Priest's torso up, and brutally twists his head to the camera. A shot, then another.

Scene 7

The family arrives in full force. A family picture.

The photographer steps up to the door and flings it open. The family dashes in, with leaping jittery movements, as though in a speeded-up film. Skipping continuously, they take their place at the bed head. A family portrait with the deceased. This taken, the family are summarily thrown out.

Scene 8

Those fresh from the battle-field: the platoon.

A platoon of conscripts about to be sent to the front are standing in the corner of the room. Pathetic, nondescript figures in full uniform, with rifles. Illegal tenants of the room since childhood, they arrive from the past, reduced to the single pose and single moment of a photograph. There is something rudimentary about these dwellers on the margins of life and memory.

Scene 9

A fine way of servicing a photographic camera: martial style.

The Photographer moves a few steps away from the spectral platoon right to the edge of the stage. The camera now points at the soldiers. While checking and adjusting the mechanism, the Photographer cannot help giggling. She turns a knob on the side: a thick barrel emerges. She presses a hidden button and a thin barrel pops out of the thick one, aiming straight at the platoon. The Photographer roars with laughter. Since all this takes place in the Big Top, she has a special treat for the soldiers: the camera turns into a machine gun.

Scene 10

Eternity, or a souvenir picture from 'Ricordo'.

Every shot is a salvo of machine gun fire. The soldiers, who have just shown slight signs of becoming mobile, freeze.

Scene 11

Discreet exit of the local photographer

The Photographer, clearly pleased with herself and her ingenuity, exits laughing hideously.

Scene 12

On the other side.

PRIEST

Although laid out and clad for the last resting place, he keeps moving. He sits up, looks around, recognizes his room, then directs his gaze towards the door which has just closed after the Photographer. Speaking to himself.

**Nobody.
Yet someone surely was here
just now?**

Not in the least surprised at the sight of the

soldiers, he catches sight of Father—
Helka's husband—in the front row.

**. . . It's about time they were
wed.**

As if in a dream. Decides to 'summon'
Father, as in a wedding ceremony. Wriggling
on the death-bed, he holds out his hand to
Father.

. . . Marian Kantor

Repeating.

Marian Kantor

No response. The Priest drags himself out of
bed and totters up to the platoon. He
scrutinizes Father, in the front row, who
appears to be dead. He lifts him up, lays the
rifle aside for him. Tries to set him on his
feet: Father topples over. He tries once
again. In the end he sets Father upright. He
peers at him with suspicion. All these
operations are accompanied by a military
march: *The Grey Infantry*. The volume of the
tune increases. The Priest disappears behind
the door only to come back carrying a huge
wooden cross on his shoulders as at
Golgotha. He is bent under its weight.

Scene 13

Father receives patient tuition in that special kind of walk known as 'marching'.

The Priest urges Father to march. He begins
to march himself, bent under the weight of
the cross. *The Grey Infantry* blares out. In
the end Father's feet indeed begin to move.
He trips over. He becomes disheartened,
'dies' again, then makes a new effort. In this
laborious manner they reach the edge of the
stage or the room. The Priest with the cross
marches on his own, passes close by the

audience, moving his free arm briskly and throwing his feet forward. Pleased with himself, he becomes one with the march. Finally he takes the cross from his shoulders and lays it against the chair, apparently remembering something. He goes to the hall where the dead bride lies on the ground in her veil. She is all in white. He tries to prop her up, drags her along, then lifts her stiff body up and places her next to Father like a doll.

Scene 14

Posthumous nuptials.

PRIEST

The time is ripe to conduct the ceremony. He reaches for the Marriage Service in the pocket of his gown.

Marian Kantor!
Wilt thou take this woman
Helena Berger
to thy wedded wife to live
together
after God's ordinance in the
holy
estate of Matrimony?

FATHER

Remains still. His face is completely lifeless. Only his legs, already propelled in the marching exercise, keep moving on the same spot. All that can be heard is the thud of his boots.

PRIEST

Prompting.

I will.

FATHER

Something like a gobble comes out of him; his teeth rattle.

PRIEST

He moves to the other side, slightly reassured.

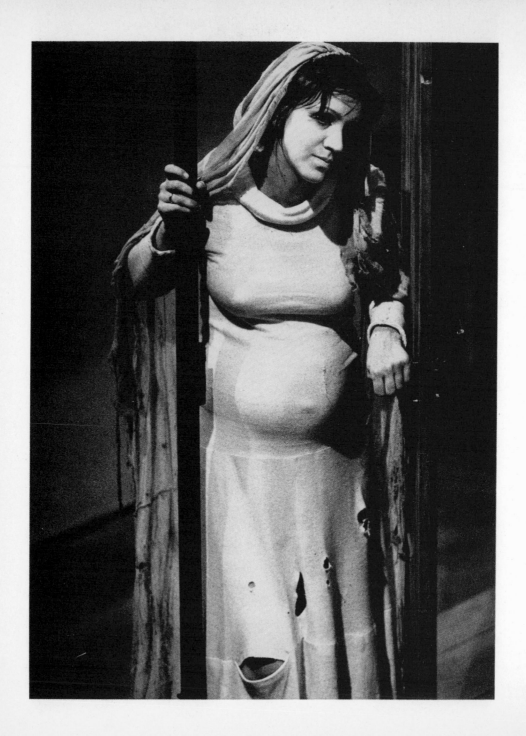

**And you, Helena
Berger, wilt thou take
Marian Kantor
to thy wedded
husband to
live together after
God's
ordinance in the holy
estate
of Matrimony?**

MOTHER HELKA

I will.

A wooden, puppet-like voice.

PRIEST

Returning to Father's side.

**I, Marian Kantor,
take you Helena Berger
to my wedded wife
to love and to cherish
till death us do part,
so grant me Lord Almighty,
in the Holy Trinity one and only
with all the saints.**

He urges Father to repeat after him. But this
lifeless dummy can utter nothing but a
hideous animal gibber, choking with the
effort of remembering the human voice.
Thus unfolds the dialogue of the quick and
the dead.
He passes over the other side to the Bride,
finding it much easier there. The wooden
voice of the Bride merges with the weary,
professional voice of the Priest.

**I, Helena Berger,
take you, Marian,
to my lawful wedded husband
to love and to cherish
to honour and obey
till death us do part.
So grant me, Lord Almighty,
in the Holy Trinity one and only
with all the saints.**

Binding the wrists of Father and Mother
Helka with a stole, the Priest pauses for a
moment.

Scene 15

And so they set off on the path of life.

The ceremony is over. Father takes hold of the Bride's hand. He walks ahead of her, dragging her along, more and more violently. The white veil trails behind, like a sign of doom. The black stole falls on the ground. They walk over it.

ACT TWO

VILIFICATION

Scene 1

A long journey across the room.

A lull. The door opens slowly, showing the Family: both Uncles, both Aunts, Grandma, Mother Helka, Adaś; people jumbled together with objects, clutching their belongings. Squeezed together, they shout in panic, a ghastly procession of yelling wrecks, who simultaneously may or may not be a group of circus actors. They cross the short distance between the door and the other end of the room as if on a long journey fraught with ambushes and perils, beset with delays and arguments.

UNCLE KAROL	**Up there.**
AUNTIE MAŃKA	**Karol!**
AUNTIE JÓZKA	**Olek!**

UNCLE OLEK	**Adaś, where are you?**
UNCLE KAROL	**My suitcase!**
UNCLE OLEK	**Where are the aunts?**
UNCLE KAROL	**Józka, keep an eye on Mańka, will you?**
AUNTIE JÓZKA	**Straight on.**
AUNTIE MAŃKA	**Stick with us, please.**
UNCLE KAROL	**Not far now.**
UNCLE OLEK	**Now, let's turn left.**
AUNTIE MAŃKA	**That's not the right way.**
AUNTIE JÓZKA	**This way, this way!**
AUNTIE MAŃKA	**And I heard the eagle in the sky calling with a great voice: woe, woe . . .**
UNCLE KAROL	**Please, Mańka, you aren't in your own house.**
AUNTIE JÓZKA	**There she goes again. It's all because of this Mańka. She's a pain in the neck, a raving lunatic.**
UNCLE OLEK	**Adaś, mind how you go.**
UNCLE KAROL	**I only hope we shall make it to the other side while it's still light.**
MOTHER HELKA	**But it's already quite dark, isn't it?**
UNCLE OLEK	**Hush, hush, hush.**
UNCLE KAROL	**Stand still.**
GRANDMA	

She sings.

	The Lord said unto my Lord, sit thou at my right hand . . .
AUNTIE JÓZKA	**Just stop moaning, you'll bring disaster.**
AUNTIE MAŃKA	**Crucify him, crucify him!**
UNCLE OLEK	**Stop going on about crosses!**
MOTHER HELKA	**Crosses, crosses everywhere.**
UNCLE KAROL	**Look, we're nearly there. There's the graveyard!**

At last they reach the other end of the room. They cling to the table like grim death.

Scene 2

The funny business of repetition.
The door, or Uncle Karol's weakness.

UNCLE KAROL   Clearly suffering from a headache, moaning.

      My head is killing me.
      Adaś. I must go out.
      If only I could get this door
      open.

      Adaś dashes to the door. Karol runs
      towards the door, then changes his mind.
      In a sudden moment of panic he turns back,
      sits down and clutches his head.

AUNTIE JÓZKA   **When will you make up your**
      mind?

      She is leaning on the table, completely worn
      out.

Scene 3

Uncle Olek's struggle with a chair.

UNCLE OLEK   Cautiously opening the door, he steps up to
      the chair, saying,

      The chair . . .

      He stares at the chair, in which Auntie Józka
      sits, half-leaning on the table, her knees wide
      apart, as if she was dead. Tearfully, he turns
      to Uncle Karol.

      Shall I sit down?
      Shan't I?
      Shall I go out?

      He tiptoes out.
      Covering her face.

AUNTIE MAŃKA
      I can't stand the sight of him.

	Oh Lord, how agonizing. Józka! Is he gone?	
AUNTIE JÓZKA	**No, he's still here.**	Dashes away. Off stage.
AUNTIE MAŃKA	**Merciful God!**	Still off stage.

The last two scenes, *The door, or Uncle Karol's weakness* and *Uncle Olek's struggle with the chair*, are motifs which recur alongside later scenes. Both represent what I call 'funny business', which often finds its way into the production: all those resurgent memories, all those comings and goings that are denied their habitual role in life, maliciously divorced from their function and *raison d'être*, because of some obscure, shadowy agency — all those actions, then, which are made to stray from the regular track of TIME and become subjected to the ceaseless workings of the VOID. There, of course, they come within easy reach of Eternity, Insanity and Death, and yet remain — trivial routines as they are — on the edge of sheer tomfoolery. . . . 'He goes out *continuously*'. Indeed the idea of 'perpetual activity' kept haunting me. And I always felt that to grasp it I ought to remain within the scope of the GAME — on the edge of tomfoolery — rather than venture into anything mechanical, 'scientific', and therefore crude.

Scene 4

You cannot just repeat one thing in life, and hope to get away with it. If you meddle with time, it will wreak its revenge. Grandma and the unburied Priest, or the unholy reduplication of the Priest's death.

GRANDMA

Pulling along the Priest's body, she tries to find a suitable place to lay it out. The rest of the family remain unruffled. However, when she turns towards the table, obviously intending to dispose of her precious burden, those sitting around break into unanimous protest.

AUNTIE JÓZKA   **Get out.**
UNCLE KAROL   **Clear off.**
AUNTIE MAŃKA   As though to a dog.
                     Put it down.
                     Who do you think you are?
UNCLE KAROL   **Just leave him where he was.**
                     Let go of him.
AUNTIE MAŃKA   **The whole house stinks.**
                     How disgraceful!

Scene 5

The Doubles — Reduplicated beings. An ambiguous hierarchy: Dummies which are almost alive and Actors who are only alive in retrospect. The audience alone are truly living.

Grandma drops the Priest (a wax figure) on the floor near the bed and darts out. In an instant she is back, carrying the Priest — Actor, who this time is vested in a glistening cassock suitable for the coffin as opposed to the shroud that the former wears. She seats him next to the wax figure.

AUNTIE MAŃKA

Rushes to the Priest and quickly kisses him on his sleeve.

Scene 6

Domestic machinations, or the delusive return of Father-on-Leave.

Scene 7

Mother Helka and her frustrated encounters.

FATHER-ON-LEAVE	Suddenly shows up, wearing an army uniform, with a rifle and a suitcase. Father keeps marching, clearly having forgotten how to make use of his feet in any other way. A certain odd pattern can be grasped behind his marching: he gets worked up, apparently because he has hit upon what seems to him a good idea — his face beaming with a positive, if not a noble, resolve; yet a little later he changes his mind, he gets discouraged for some obscure reason, dismayed. On such occasions his face takes on a malevolent look, twisted by the horrible mental processes working behind it.
MOTHER HELKA	Coming forward, as if about to greet him, she changes her mind and goes back. This is repeated several times, long enough for the tenants to develop an interest in these peculiar and more and more equivocal comings and goings.
UNCLE KAROL	**Marian, what on earth brings you here?**
AUNTIE MAŃKA	**Oh, Helka, you poor thing! How could he ditch you like that . . .**
AUNTIE JÓZKA	**Obviously he lost all sense of shame.**
UNCLE OLEK	Opening the door, bumps into Father-on-

Leave. He steps back and beckons to Uncle
Karol who sits at the table.

	Karol!
	Who is this fellow?
UNCLE KAROL	**Marian is back.**
UNCLE OLEK	**Shall I go out?**
	See you at the corner.

He slips out, trying to efface himself,
immediately returning. This time he runs
into Mother Helka, who glides forward like a
sleep-walker, still in her white wedding veil.

	Karol?
	Who is that?
UNCLE KAROL	**This is Helka.**
AUNTIE MAŃKA	**The image of Helka!**
UNCLE OLEK	

He goes out, but instantly comes back.

Whose Helka?
Marian's?
Shall I go out?
Had I better go out?
I'll wait at the corner.
Karol!
**Where's the postcard that
came yesterday?**
**Didn't it say he was killed in
action?**
I'll be at the corner.

Scene 8

A family of Comedians show their solidarity.

Father-on-Leave's incessant marching
becomes more and more annoying.
Expediency coupled with the intruder's
barrack-room language mobilize the Family
against him. They encircle the deranged
Helka. Getting more and more worked up,
they mount a show of jeering and sneering in

front of the marching Father-on-Leave, who
in turn gets more and more worked up,
becoming increasingly abusive.
(Uncle Karol, Uncle Olek, Auntie Mańka,
Auntie Józka, Grandma, Adaś and Mother
Helka in the middle.)

FAMILY

We must join forces
against this scum.
We can't stand for this.
We'll show him
we stay in line
and won't let him get his way,
that we'll stand by her
as a family . . .
Scum, just scum.
When he first came over
he had nothing but a set of
whiskers.
Well, what did he have?
What then?
Had he got anything?
Had he got a thing?
Helka went on and on about
him having something . . .
What was it?
He had what he had.
So he was given a job . . .
And with her dowry,
everything . . .
Just everything!
Two brass beds,
and piqué quilts
and mattresses stuffed with
horse hair,
two wardrobes with mirrors,
an oak dresser,
and what about the palm-tree,
and those bamboo whatnots?
Also a carpet,
no, two carpets!
and a wall-hanging with a swan
over the bed!
table-cloths, a set of china,
a compote-service and a 24-

carat gold watch,
shirts, underwear,
and didn't we have shoes made
to measure for him,
and a black wedding suit?
And look at him . . .
What about him?
Him, him, him.
Just nothing, nothing.
He had nothing.
Just a down-and-out.

Scene 9

Helka on Golgotha.

Scene 10

Crown of thorns. The vilification of Helka.

The family of Comedians exceeds all bounds. Their jeering begins to turn in on itself — an activity performed for its own sake. Gradually they direct their outpourings at Mother Helka. Swayed by their own frenzy, they withdraw to the hall, shut the door, then quickly return to bring the scene to an end. Mother Helka can now be seen sitting on Golgotha, a kind of mobile scaffold, or if you wish, just a push-cart. The family keep pushing this thing with Mother Helka on it, her knees apart, she looks like a dummy. Mad Mańka begins to speak in the words of the Gospels, as she does whenever a crisis befalls this terrible family. She puts a crown of thorns upon the head of the Insane and Sorrowful Mother Helka. Some sort of *de-collage* is being enacted, in which tragedy and circus clowning are merged. Quite in keeping with the style of the play, another, not the last, reference to the Gospels emerges. The family vilifies Mother Helka, sneering and spitting.

FAMILY	Oh, Helka, Helka! Why did he degrade you and so meanly desert you . . . Perhaps it serves you right to be so degraded, debased, defiled and abused. How are the mighty fallen!
MAD AUNTIE MAŃKA	Oh, oh, oh, when the morning was come, Pilate had him scourged, they put a crown of thorns upon his head.
FAMILY	. . . and they spat upon him and mocked him and smote him on the head and the kidneys. Oh, wretched Helka, Wretch indeed, you have come to this in the end.
MAD AUNTIE MAŃKA	Oh, oh, oh, they cried out:
FAMILY	Crucify him, crucify him.
MAD AUNTIE MAŃKA	Oh, oh, oh, then said they all, Art thou the Son of God?
FAMILY	He hath spoken blasphemy! He is guilty of death!
AUNTIE MAŃKA	Why, what evil hath he done?
FAMILY	They smote him, they smote him upon the head, spat and smote on him . . . Oh, Helka, Helka, poor Helka. Nobody will feel sorry for you!

You must have sinned a lot,
and your conscience is . . .
Józka, what went on with your
Olek?
Oh Helka, you must be guilty . . .
Olek! Now you say nothing!
You deserve to be mocked,
don't you?
Yes, mocked,
and debased, rejected,
abandoned!
Come let us spit upon you,
abuse and sneer at you,
and defile you,
and WASH OUR HANDS!

Scene 11

The dead soldiers have fun.

For some time the platoon has been
advancing from all corners of the room with
the same clumsy, random movements. . . .
Falling and getting up, they gradually
encircle the Family and Mother Helka on
Golgotha. It seems they'll be trampled
underfoot at any minute. Holding their rifles
in the air, the soldiers stagger and walk into
everything in their way. The Family recede
from view. Suddenly Mother Helka, as a
Dummy, appears above the soldiers' heads.

Scene 12

Helka as a dummy.

The soldiers have fun with Helka. They cast her high into the air, and she falls — arms and legs shamelessly flung apart — into her dirty, tattered wedding veil, which the soldiers stretch out beneath her. They walk slowly from the room and disappear behind the door, leaving Helka on the floor: dead, raped, her knees apart.

Scene 13

Pilate

The Photographer's Widow, a factotum's role in the production, strides in. Pausing over Helka's body, she stretches out her hands and wipes them with a grimy rag.

Scene 14

The Second Wedding.

All the time Father-on-Leave keeps marching, showing not the slightest sign of fatigue. The unfolding events do not appear to affect him in the least. He now turns to

Mother Helka, lifts her in his arms, and as in
Act One, carries her, pacing with his crisp
march step. As before, the tune of *The Grey
Infantry* is heard.

Scene 15

The Priest.

Important moments in the life of the Family
inevitably demand the Priest's presence. So
here he waits, on the edge of the stage for
Father-on-Leave, who carries Mother Helka
in his arms. As before, Father has crossed the
boundaries of the stage to join the audience.
Now he is on his way back. But there is
another character who faithfully, if at a
distance, follows the family in their turmoil.
You would not expect him to be missing on
this occasion. The Deportee — Uncle Stasio
— shows up in the doorway with his violin
case. He begins to turn the crank. The same
carol as before, strangely mutilated . . . .
Once the first familiar grinding tones are
heard, Father-on-Leave roughly flings
Mother Helka's body over his shoulder, her
head and veil trailing behind. The Priest
leads the dismal couple on. Everybody
vanishes behind the door, but of course I am
there to shut it after them.

ACT THREE

CRUCIFIXION

Scene 1

The Family moving back into the same room, lugging along the indispensible accessories of their daily existence. Both Uncles, both Aunts, Grandma, Mother Helka, Father-on-Leave, Adaś. They arrive at their old place by the window to sit there again, happily, like cocks on a dunghill.

Scene 2

The doubles reconciled.

The Priest, still unburied, is in his mortuary gown, barefoot, a black biretta on his head. A motionless corpse that Grandma brings in and seats in a chair near the table. This done, she turns to the Double of the Priest that leans against the bed on the floor, picks him up and seats him next to the first. The two will be sitting thus, elbow-to-elbow, menacingly alike, with an air of anticipation of something conclusive to take place about them. Their stillness broods over this room which *exists not*.

Scene 3

The repetition of the commonplace: if you knew how to compress the bulk of calendar time, you would no longer be able to dodge the encounter with eternity and death. The Primer of dressing.

The sequence consists of two twin and simultaneous actions which unfold a number of times in reverse order to each other. The two actors who perform these are doubles: they appear as a multiplication of one person. Every action has a short text to it which can be repeated several times, its content reflecting an activity simultaneously occurring in reverse.

UNCLE OLEK *busy dressing:*
A hat
A hat on my head
Off I go with a hat on!

A waistcoat under a jacket
Though lacking a jacket
under a coat
Off I go with a waistcoat on!

A coat on a jacket
Though lacking a jacket
on a waistcoat
Off I go with a coat on!

UNCLE KAROL *busy undressing:*
A hat
A hat on my head
Off I go with no hat on!

A coat
A coat on a jacket
Though lacking a jacket on a waistcoat
Off I go with no waistcoat on!

A waistcoat under a coat
Under a jacket a waistcoat
Though lacking a jacket under a coat
Off I go with no coat on!

Let us call a *round* a single full run of the Uncles' simultaneous actions. Within one round Uncle Olek must get undressed — take off a hat, a coat, a jacket and a waistcoat, and at the same time Uncle Karol must get dressed — don a hat, a waistcoat, a jacket and a coat. Whilst inside the room, the two Uncles normally keep their hats and coats on. This may be due to their unsettled circumstances, moving house over and over again etc. They are always on the move and seem to be ready to leave the house any minute. This time, however, Uncle Olek has apparently decided to stick to one place for a while. He goes up to the wardrobe, opens it, takes off his hat, coat, jacket and waistcoat, and hangs each on a hanger. He only keeps his shirt on. Having seen what the other is up to, Uncle Karol decides, fraternally, to follow suit and stay indoors as well. After all, they are never apart. He goes up to the wardrobe and takes off his hat, coat, jacket and waistcoat. However, as soon as he begins to undress, Uncle Olek has changed his mind about staying in. He would now rather go for a walk, so he dons his hat, waistcoat, jacket and coat. Absorbed in his own undressing and with his back to Uncle Olek, Uncle Karol fails to notice that Uncle Olek, by now ready to go out, performs the same operation, albeit in reverse. Only when he has undressed to his shirt does he discover that Uncle Olek has dressed and is about to leave. Loth to part with him, Uncle Karol hurriedly dons his hat, waistcoat, jacket and coat. In so doing he does not realize that in the meantime the other, devoid of will power and perpetually beset by pathological doubts as he is — losing his resolve again and again — takes his hat, coat, jacket and waistcoat off once more. Uncle Karol turning to Uncle Olek, realizes to his utter bewilderment, that Uncle Olek has changed his mind again and decided to stay at home undressed. Disillusioned, Uncle Karol takes his hat, coat, jacket and waistcoat off.

At eactly the same time, Uncle Olek by now completely exhausted, gazes around the room aghast; he decides to leave it for good. He dons his hat, waistcoat, jacket and coat. Uncle Karol, having at this very moment completed another round of undressing, turns round to find Uncle Olek fully dressed. Beset by strong doubts as to Uncle Olek's sanity, he hurriedly dons his hat, waistcoat, jacket and coat.

And so on and on, so long as you can find fresh (and comic) reasons for changes of mind . . . .

Scene 4

Forebodings of Mad Auntie Mańka.

Mad Mańka periodically goes through a religious crisis. She then pontificates, quoting from the Gospels — a sinister Cassandra counting, in this bourgeois room, the hours left before the impending catastrophe. With its perfect articulation, the voice resounds uncannily against the sudden relapses of silence that hang over the everyday activities of the inhabitants of the room, this bizarre *sanctuary*.

AUNTIE MAŃKA   **Oh, oh, oh,**
I heard the eagle in the sky
calling with a great voice: woe,
woe.

The first opening of the door.

Eight o'clock.
Ore otto.
And he asked him, saying,
art thou the king of the Jews?
They cried out:

FAMILY   **Crucify him!**
Crucify him!

AUNTIE MAŃKA

The second opening of the door.

Ten o'clock.
Ore dieci.
. . . and there arose a smoke
out of the pit,
as the smoke of a great furnace;
and there came out of the
smoke locusts upon the earth,
and unto them was given
power,
as the scorpions of the earth
have power.

The third opening of the door.

Twelve o'clock.
Ore dodici.

Scene 5

Eight o'clock! The first opening of the door.

From the very outset of the scene, inscrutable knocks and bangs can be heard behind the door; clearly, something is going on out there. The continuous noises, now louder, now softer, transport Auntie Mańka into a state of frenzy, in which she cites the Book of Revelation in that prophetic voice of hers.

AUNTIE MAŃKA **Oh, oh, oh,
I heard the eagle in the sky
calling with a great voice: woe,
woe.**

UNCLE KAROL

Interrupting his Rites of Dressing, he goes up to the door, listens to the mounting noises outside, then flings the door open. Things are happening in the hall that cannot be contained in the room, still less in the minds of the tenants: child soldiers, wearing black birettas, drag something along, completely absorbed in whatever they are doing, hard to say whether a chore or a game. The huge wooden cross, which we recognize from the first scene, can be seen. The children are caught in the process of nailing to the cross the dummy of the Priest which is dressed in the mortuary gown and a black biretta. A welter of squashed bodies. The very moment the door opens, the children scurry off and vanish, leaving the cross behind. Uncle Karol is deep in thought, slowly closing the door.
Counting the time.

AUNTIE MAŃKA
**Eight o'clock.
Ore otto!**

Scene 6

Grandma's morning exercise.

GRANDMA

Doing her morning exercise stretched out on the bed, she reminds one of a weird blackened cricket. Her black skirt is hitched up, her long thin legs are in black stockings, which tear here and there. She is stretching and bending her legs alternately. Vermin-like movements of the head, convulsive throbs. The physical decay comes over as a contrast to the abstract precision of the exercise. She pauses for a moment, then gets carried away again to the point of sheer exhaustion.

Scene 7

Ten o'clock! The second opening of the door.

AUNTIE MAŃKA

The noises behind the door have again grown louder.

**And he asked, saying:
Art thou the King of the Jews?
They cried out:**

She draws the whole family into her hallucinations.
Crying out.

FAMILY

**Crucify him!
Crucify him!**

UNCLE OLEK
AND ADAŚ

Opening the door.

Undeterred, the children continue their bizarre game. By now the cross stands upright, amidst bits of scaffolding and cords.

UNCLE OLEK

The dummy of the Priest hangs loose. The children can be seen climbing the scaffolding. Their game must have reached its climax, for everything comes to a standstill.
Erases the scene by closing the door slowly.

Scene 8

Graveyard Games.

MOTHER HELKA
AND ADAŚ

They are playing with a cross torn from a grave, which happens to be in the room. Adaś rushes to 'hide' it somewhere in a corner, himself lurking nearby, on the look-out for Helka. She for her part runs around looking for something, and finds this object — hardly suitable as a child's plaything. Now it is her turn to hide it. They spy on each other.
Thus unfolds this 'hunt the thimble', as if in a nightmare . . . .

Scene 9

Sudden arrival of Father-on-Leave with his barrack-room habits.

Meanwhile, Father-on-Leave has been sitting in a chair, motionless and lifeless, the rifle and the black suitcase at his feet. When his time has come, he stands up and sets off on his way, marching and swearing like a trooper. He opens and shuts his suitcase, taking out various blackened odds and ends of unknown origin. He scatters them all around the stage, then picks them up and sticks them in his suitcase, swearing all the time, sparing no-one's blushes. He has turned somehow rabid.

Scene 10

Twelve o'clock! The third opening of the door.

The clatter behind the door has reached a climax.
Intervening with her Revelations.

AUNTIE MAŃKA

**. . . and there arose a smoke out of the pit,
as the smoke of a great furnace;
and there came out of the smoke locusts upon the earth,
and unto them was given power,
as the scorpions of the earth have power.**

FATHER-ON-LEAVE

Fretfully marching towards the door; he opens it. The ante-room is empty, only the cross is there, the flaccid dummy of the Priest looming behind it. Father-on-Leave showers his verbiage on the Priest and furiously slams the door. Silence falls.
In her sinister voice, counting the hours:

AUNTIE MAŃKA

It's twelve o'clock.

Realizing that it is high time for her to leave the room, she rushes out in panic, pulling her chair along behind her.

Scene 11

Two Uncles line up three chairs. The elusive yet painstaking calculations are bound to prove futile. They may soon cause a bit of trouble, too.

Uncle Karol and Uncle Olek are busy making certain intriguing calculations: measuring distances by paces, or with utmost precision lining up three chairs next to one another. They also check the distance between the chairs and the two doubles, between the chairs and the door, and tread a perpendicular to the door and the footlights. At length, they sit down in two chairs, leaving the third chair *free* between them. They wait.

Scene 12

Enter Mad Auntie Mańka in a strangely familiar army uniform.

AUNTIE MAŃKA

Struts forward, from behind the wardrobe, tilting forward and backward like a puppet with a military gait. She wears a strangely familiar uniform, disguised as someone (you know who.) Mind you, we refuse to identify the uniform, or name the person, lest we feed the facile fantasies of blockheads. Indeed, true *awe* will never resort to derivative devices, it cannot be explained. *Awe* transcends our imagination. When it is there, it comes as a *premonition*.

Scene 13

'That fellow' has a problem with a chair.

The two Uncles, who have as yet neither disclosed their intentions nor made their fresh role plain to anybody, are being confronted with certain contingencies arising from military disciplines. To begin with, the game was not worked out by them in every detail, and now they have allowed themselves to be taken unawares by Mad Mańka and her ghastly transformation. For it is Mańka who is pacing before them, performing real military drill. At last she halts behind the free chair. She is held up there: the military drill does not allow for casual, non-linear movements. The Uncles move the chair a pace forward. This does not make any difference to her, though, for having taken a pace forward 'that fellow' (as we shall call this figure) finds himself now uneasily flanked by the Uncles sitting in their chairs, but still unable to sit down himself. Realizing at last that something untoward has occurred, the Uncles stand up and have a sideways talk with each other. They must have hit upon a brilliant idea for, chuckling, as they always do on such occasions, they move their two chairs simultaneously (they do everything simultaneously) backwards. Whereupon they sit down again swiftly, their faces enigmatic. We can now see what they are up to: 'that fellow', mindful of nothing but his status, will surely try to take a seat between the Uncles, and as the chair is missing there, he will inevitably find himself on the floor. A silly joke, this, yet one which will take an unexpected turn. 'That fellow' does indeed make an attempt at taking a seat there, yet instead of crashing onto the floor, he holds himself suspended at the level of the missing chair. The key to this 'miracle' must remain among the usual stock-in-trade of the Big Top. After all, safeguarding 'that fellow's' honour was not my purpose here.

Scene 14

In which the humbug of duplication is unmasked.

After the none-too-happy end of the last incident, the Uncles must embark on a new exploit. This time they feel they have worked out the scenario in the minutest detail. Yet it is not hard to see that they are only the unbriefed, even if cunning, executors of a DESIGN: never mind if the means to fulfill it look very crude; all the better, they will thus conceal the sinister end, to say nothing of the final solution. The Uncles step up to the Priest and his double. You cannot tell which of the two is alive, and which dead. Although of dubious repute themselves, the two Uncles turn into judges straight away: they will pronounce one of the two suspects guilty. In this new capacity, they are little short of becoming deputy directors of the production itself, or if you will, chief clowns of the Big Top. They serve a writ on DUPLICATION, the duplication of the original created by God and nature. It all hinges on a quaint metaphysical game played by children. The one of the two who is found to be alive will be pronounced guilty. The judges must present the evidence. Uncle Karol craftily raises the right arm of one of the two 'Priests'. The other 'Priest' does exactly the same: his arm rises. So far this tells the Uncles nothing, they

are too dim-witted. Now they raise one
'Priest's' left leg. The other 'Priest' raises his.
They are unaware of any differences between
the two. Now we know that they are idiots.
Still they begin to harbour increasing
suspicions about the latter. They hurriedly
work out a new strategy. This time they are
convinced of being in the right: they snatch a
biretta off the head of the second 'Priest'.
The first does not move. So the other is the
LIVING ORIGINAL, no doubt about that. Thus
the LIVE ONE is guilty. This is all very strange.
The two idiots appear to be but a tool of some
higher power or faculty. The two are unable
to comprehend the GUILT of creating a
sacrilegious verisimilitude in MAN's image.
(For a better explanation see my comments
in the Director's Notes.) The two Uncles,
turning from judges into EXECUTIONERS,
grab the Priest.

Scene 15

Court Martial.

The Uncles set the Priest upright, back to the
audience, downstage, treating him as a
convict. They sit down in the chairs flanking
'that fellow', each holding a rattle.

Now, wooden rattles replace bells, when
these are banned during Holy Week.
Incidentally, as Professor Jan Kott testifies,
rattles are called 'horloges de la mort' in
various localities. Their wooden clatter, fitful
and hollow, is redolent of the realm of death.
Small wonder that the three equivocal judges
will use them in their sinister practices. 'That
fellow' strikes his rattle just once, and with

no great enthusiasm, but the Uncles shake theirs with great fervour, many times over. Each time they strike, the Priest recoils, bends his knees and collapses.

Scene 16

Two o'clock!

GRANDMA

Time passes. Now it is Grandma who, after lying dead — just human remains — rises, and amid total silence announces:

Two o'clock!

Scene 17

Drills in killing.

The two Uncles jump to their feet, violently pick up the recumbent Priest and set him upright. They flank him as guards or turnkeys would a condemned man.

The door opens wide. A squad with fixed bayonets can be seen. They advance. The sounds of *The Grey Infantry* march. Grandma, at the end of her tether, rises once again.

GRANDMA   **Ten minutes left!**

The soldiers come forward. Each buries his bayonet in the Priest's body. The Priest totters. Then, one after another, they step backward to the door and vanish through the gap.

Scene 18

They go and fetch that object. They will all carry it in.

Here comes the platoon; drunk, wild soldiers dragging the cross, ladders, cords, as well as an object called Golgotha.

Scene 19

The object called Golgotha. Five minutes left!

The crude wooden structure labelled Golgotha is a scaffold. They set it up in a great rush. They sink the heavy cross into the object called Golgotha.
Grandma exclaims with her last breath.

GRANDMA

Five minutes left!

The Uncles, acting as guards and executioners, hunt the Priest down like an animal, and put the cross on his shoulders. The Priest crawls under its weight until he collapses, then the executioners manage to put it on Mother Helka. When she collapses under its weight as well, they grab at little Adaś, who is now to become their victim and the villain of the piece.

Scene 20

And so it came to pass. Three o'clock!

> Adaś is hunted down and forced to climb Golgotha. He spreads his arms. A pitiful sight, in his new school uniform: a white, stiff collar, a necktie and a pair of long trousers for the first time in his life.

Scene 21

The wooden bells of death.

> The soldiers withdraw little by little. All of the Family get hold of the rattles and start shaking them like mad in a toneless rattle of lamentation. They all retreat, but the rattles continue to be heard off stage for a long time.

Scene 22

Descent from the cross. Świątek: the Polish wayside figure of Our Lord the Sorrowful.

> Slowly the Priest rises to his feet. He looks round, steps up to the cross, helps Adaś down, places him on the ground, straightens his jacket for him, and, with much tenderness, sends him away. Then he sits down at the foot of the cross, rests his distressed head upon his arm, and so he remains.

ACT FOUR

ADAŚ IS SENT TO THE FRONT

Scene 1

Yet another of their endless moves.

The wardrobe is abruptly flung open. The whole Family jumps out of it. It was not at all unusual in those days for common objects to change their function all of a sudden. The Family as ever on the move, terror-stricken, searches for help.

UNCLE KAROL	**There's no place like home!**
GRANDMA	**It's all right, all right dear,**
KATARZYNA	**provided we stick together.**
MINGLED	**Karol! Olek!**
VOICES	**Mańka! Józka!**
HELKA	**Crosses, crosses everywhere!**
UNCLE KAROL	**Hush, Helka, you are not in your own house.**
AUNTIE MAŃKA	**Józka, where's Adaś?**
AUNTIE JÓZKA	**Adaś, Adaś!**
MOTHER HELKA	**Adaś.**

Scene 2

Adaś is enlisted.

At last he can convey a piece of auspicious news to the Family.

UNCLE KAROL	**Adaś has got his marching orders.**

Scene 3

The family huddle round the table as usual. Uncle Karol is the patriot. Uncle Olek is an old skiver. Aunt Józka has no respect for death in the field. Aunt Mańka is an expert on Revelations, and talks of nothing else.

A pause. The table abruptly tilts to one side, like the deck of a life boat or a ship sinking in a stormy sea. The room is hardly a safe anchorage any longer. They cling to the table and try to outshout the roar of the waves, you do not know why or for whose benefit. They are pictures of deathly terror. (This terror must come across as 'separate' from the things they say.)

Adaś is missing. He will reappear later, much later. The family are now voicing their different opinions about war. Uncle Karol, a loyal citizen, Uncle Olek, a typical dodger, Aunt Józka has no regard whatsoever for 'dying for one's country', Aunt Mańka sees the situation in terms of apocalyptic declamation.

UNCLE KAROL

Refusing to become affected by the others' reactions, carries on, enthusiastic, persuasive, choking yet increasingly eloquent.

**Adaś has his marching orders!
He has been called up!
Perhaps not a hero yet,
but his deeds are already
heroic!
A hero!
Our pride and joy!**

AUNTIE MAŃKA

Joining in with her Revelations.

**And I looked and heard
the eagle in the sky
calling with a great voice: woe,
woe . . .**

UNCLE KAROL

Choking with rapture.

Adaś!
our pride,
our glorious, invincible one,
our emperor and monarch,
our fatherland,
we all unaided,
to our last breath,
we the old guard,
we . . .

UNCLE OLEK   Well, something must be done
to help him out,
to obtain his release,
we'll have to think of
something,
make him stay put, maybe,
just watching the world go by
or doing a bit of gardening . . .
No, better indoors,
if he doesn't poke his head out . . .

AUNTIE JÓZKA   The best idea is medical
grounds,
say varicose veins,
he has got varicose veins,
hasn't he?
They can't push him out there
to die!
Who is responsible for this?
For his death?
Who? Who?

AUNTIE MAŃKA   . . . and there arose the smoke
out of the pit
as the smoke of a great furnace
and there came out of the
smoke
locusts upon the earth
and unto them was given power
as the scorpions of the earth
have power.

UNCLE KAROL   What have varicose veins to do
with war?
We are all under one banner!
On the pages of history!
We shall not give in!
Forward march!

		He chokes.
UNCLE OLEK	. . . best of all keep him at home, or else in the hospital, yes, there, let's get him to the hospital, into a bed, the right sort of illness, or a bit of amputation, or maybe typhoid, let's save him with typhoid!	
AUNTIE JÓZKA		Shouting.
	Amputation? His head off? His leg off? Off he goes altogether? All of him away? Passed away? Killed in action? Mixed with the mud? Our Adaś! Adaś! Adaś!	
		Urging him to hurry up.

Scene 4

Adaś is late. Perhaps we are already at the railway station.

Scene 5

It looks as if there has been a time-shift and Adaś has met his glorious death in the field.

Although the Family are still sitting at the table united as ever, their shouts of 'Adaś!, Adaś!, hurry up' apparently directed at the conscripted Adaś, recede and fade away.

Scene 6

The Priest, who passed away long ago, brings in a conscript's suitcase and a rifle — all that remains of Adaś.

He lays the remnants down, next to a grave with a cross, earth piled up in the room. The priest moves out, as if he had forgotten something.

Scene 7

The Deportee-cum-busker (Uncle Stasio) turns up as usual at a difficult moment.

Outwardly a violin-playing busker (see my note on *The Deportee-Violinist*), Uncle Staś has got nothing left but a violin case, in which he conceals a hurdy-gurdy. He turns the crank of the machine with a touch of self-consciousness if not pain. A tragically mutilated version of the carol from Chopin's b-minor scherzo emerges from the case.
In the context of the Big Top, a bit of hackneyed pathos triggers off a crude though genuine emotion.

Scene 8

A hearse.

> The Priest comes back, with the same cross.
> The cross, slanting, is fixed to a flimsy
> trolley. The Priest pushes the cross forward
> the way you would push a bike. The body of
> Adaś is stretched on this cross-mobile.
> Cautiously, the Priest takes the body of Adaś
> down and lays it on the ground. Incidentally,
> this section links up with a much later
> close-up, where Adaś will be lying dead on a
> field furrowed by shells.

Scene 9

In the room of my childhood all the trains travel East.

> The back of the room has sliding walls made
> of coarse planks, not unlike those you might
> see used for a wretched (railway) shack.
> When, a little later, the walls slide open
> showing a gap shut off by a wooden barrier,
> the wretched shack will all of a sudden turn
> into a cattle wagon. In it, Adaś's body will be
> carried off together with the others. For the
> time being the walls are shut.

Scene 10

Inferno.

The Priest walks to the back of the stage, stops at the door, listens, and abruptly opens it. A cattle wagon, one of those in which conscripts were taken to the front line. There are lots of conscripts inside huddled together; levelled down, united by a common fate. An entangled seething mass merged in an almost animal democracy, in an eruption of some kind of primal herd instinct if not sexual euphoria. A gross, obscene display of bodies jumbled higgledy-piggledy with the naked wax figures of conscripted convicts.

Scene 11

The Priest and his Requiem.

Into this dumb hell throbbing with debauchery the old Priest flings the body of poor Adaś. Then, as if mechanically, from deep-seated habit, he casts earth on him, as on a freshly-dug grave. Movements devout, meticulous.

Scene 12

Their farewell.

The family runs alongside the train.
Moving on the spot, as though in a film, they
wave their handkerchiefs. Shouts. The Priest
slowly closes the door to the 'inferno', as if he
was closing the door of the tabernacle.

ACT FIVE

THE LAST SUPPER

Scene 1

In which the death-bed machine wreaks moral havoc among the Family.

The death-bed is a piece of machinery, a
revolving machine of death. The top, made
of unplaned boards, can rotate around a
shaft, which ends in cog-wheels and a crank.
As the top is made to rotate, each of its sides
becomes alternately the upper or the under
side. On one side of the top lies the DUMMY
of the Priest. Attached to the other side there
is an ACTOR playing the Priest. The Family
splits into two small groups. First group:
Uncle Karol, Grandma, Aunt Mańka take
the side of the Actor-Priest. Second group:
Uncle Olek, Aunt Józka, Mother Helka on
the side of the Dummy-Priest.

Situation 1. The Dummy on top

GROUP ONE	GROUP TWO
that's not him	such a loss have we endured
that's not the real one	for ever in our remembrance
he's not one of us	in peace may he rest
he's somebody else's	we the successors
that's not our Uncle	he our provider
why should we grieve for another	the inheritance ours
a transplant	holy holy
a replacement	let candles be lit
neither real nor one of us	and a mass said to his memory

Creeping on the floor they peep under the bed and talk to the deceased underneath.

our reverend one	of blessed memory
our provider	holy holy holy
such a loss have we endured	with all the saints
Karol go on turning	in peace may he rest
round and round and round	may the earth lie lightly
	on him

As they turn the crank round, the Dummy gradually sinks while the Actor emerges from underneath.

oh oh oh look here he comes	oh he's climbing away
the head	oh how they turn
the head has got through	those turncoats
we have got him wholly	our own kith and kin
unharmed and undamaged	all's as good as lost
one of us and wholly ours	all's as good as lost

Situation 2. The Actor on top

Kneeling and peeping under the bed.

we won't let you go	they keep putting you down
we will lay you out	they keep turning you down
bury you nice and cool	
remember you for ever	prevaricating as they please
lay wreaths and flowers	but we shall stand by you
light candles	ever and ever with you
have a mass said	and give everything to you
may you rest in peace	wreaths and flowers and candles

They keep turning, and the Dummy surfaces.

oh oh oh look how they turn
they have stolen a march on us
the turncoats
our own kith and kin
let's hold out against that lot
and kneel down all of us
around him

we shall pull you through
bury you nice and warm
but never forget you
Olek go on turning
let's have him on top
round and round and round

Situation 3.   The Dummy on top

Kneeling they address the deceased under the bed

they trod you down
showed no regard
gave you such trouble
took no pity on you
so have no pity on them
not a scrap

here he comes again
weary and weak
and yet quite whole
even if wholly dead
thanks be to God
may he rest in peace
may he be blessed
with all the saints

They begin to turn the crank.

we mustn't give in
Karol give our
provider a turn
Mańka watch the
crank
turn, turn, turn
let's hold them back

oh, here they go again
Olek! Józka!

he slips away
he leaves us
that one is not one of us

Situation 4.   The Actor on top

my head is turning
is he one of us?
may he rest in peace
holy holy
wreaths and flowers
have a mass said

we must never confuse
our lot with theirs
let's hold them back
round and round

They go on turning, the Dummy coming up.

Situation 5.   The Dummy on top

here they go again
my head's turning

there's hope
he'll be back

he is not one of ours
it's not him
what does it matter
up and down up and down

They go on turning, the Actor appears.

Olek, here they go again
hold it firm
look how they turn
those turncoats
to the crank!
let's hold them back

And so on and on, the turning becoming increasingly fast.

FAMILY

At last they jointly drag the Priest down, brutally and unceremoniously pull him all ways, then, loth to be bothered with him any longer, drop him on the floor and swiftly exit. All this is inexplicable and absurd.

Scene 2

The Priest remains alone, though not for too long.

The Priest alone, dropped on the floor. Yet he soon rises again, battered and utterly worn out. He goes to the door, and is about to open it, when the door opens by itself, pushed from outside.

Scene 3

Unexpected entrance of the actors.

We are to witness another imperfect repetition — imperfect, for nothing can be revived from the past with absolute exactness. The Dummy-Doubles have their own, not quite reputable, part in the incident. After all, art is always a counterfeit. Which gives it its measure of profundity and of tragic fascination. Storming into the room are the Family together with the Child-Soldiers wearing priests' birettas and carrying rifles with fixed bayonets. They pull a huge cross along, and the Dummy of the Priest. The Child-Comedians' game has gone a bit too far. There is no stopping it. We may as well let things come to a head, in this way, through the welter of events and confusion of facts, towards an irrevocable outcome.

Scene 4

At last a 'decent', albeit hurried, funeral for the Priest.

The room of my childhood becomes a scene of GRAND TURMOIL, bordering on sheer lunacy. Brutally and sadistically, the gang of Child-Comedians nail the Dummy-Double of the Priest to the cross. One of the soldiers, the biggest one — almost a giant — lifts the cross with the Dummy onto his shoulder and starts marching. Toddling briskly after his own double is the Dead Priest. He bids a

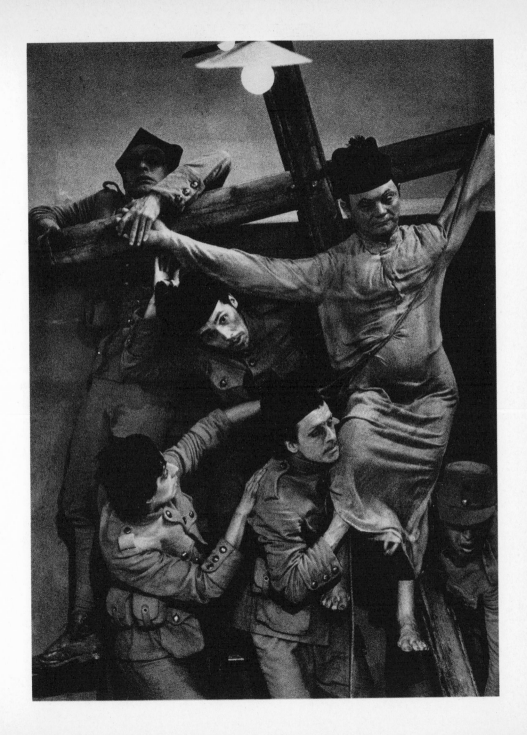

plaintive farewell to the Family, gathered here in full force, in a typical funeral procession. As usual, the platoon monitors events, their role obscure at the moment. All this happens in an incomprehensible rush. The procession moves on in a circle, a vicious circle. The soldiers' march blends with the Psalm.

Scene 5

The Celebrations are marred by an unexpected occurrence. The Little Rabbi, his music-hall 'funeral' song and his subsequent, much later, fate.

From behind the scenes, the Little Rabbi darts out unexpectedly, a marionette-like figure in synagogue garment. Running up to this weird procession, he catches up with the Priest who follows the Coffin-Cross. Wringing his hands in despair he sings his music-hall 'funeral' song.

THE RABBI

**SHA SHA SHA DE REBE
GITE
SHA SHA SHA DE REBE
STITE
SHA SHA SHA BAM REBEN
STITE
DER SHAMES BA DY TUR
IN DI REBEZN OY IS DUIS A
REBIZIN
OY OY OY
OY OY OY
OY OY OY OY OY OY OY
OY OY OY OY
OY OY OY OY
OY OY OY OY OY OY OY OY
OY OY OY
OY OY OY
OY OY OY OY OY**

In the end the soldiers have had enough. They take aim in a flash. The firing squad do their work. The wretched Little Rabbi falls down (the full significance of this image will only emerge later). The Priest lifts the Little Rabbi. The Little Rabbi takes up his song again. Another volley, the Little Rabbi collapses, and so it goes on, a number of times, repeated as things are in my theatre. Then the Rabbi leaves for ever.

Scene 6

The end of the game.

Like any other game, the funeral procession fades away. The Family disappear in the doorway, the Soldiers fall down, as if dead.

Scene 7

'That fellow' again.

Another effigy emerges from behind the scenes, a pretty hideous figure this time. However, it is just Mad Aunt Mańka, who, it will be remembered, has a taste for disguises. Her frequent transformations leave the Family dumbfounded. This time she wears the uniform which I call The Uniform-of-You-Know-Who. She marches. Soldier's boots thud on the floor in the total quiet of the room. 'That fellow' utters commands in

an unknown language, that sounds like a dog barking. (A comment apparently made about the language of the Huns and Attila by Caesar's officers.)

'THAT FELLOW' **MARSHUTEM MEHTI HURAM MARSHUTEM MEHTI HURAM MEHRAM TEHURI HIREM HIREM TEHURI MARCHUTEM HAU HAU HAU etc.**

The Soldiers rise and collapse. Each marching, paying no attention to the other, they whirl and leap with fishy eyes, convulsive cataleptic twitches, showing no will of their own. 'That fellow' keeps marching too, throwing his legs up in the air, tilting backward and forward like a puppet, fiercely, with increasing ardour, shouting commands. In the end, he has no choice but to quit all the buffoonery and go out. As if relieved by his exit, the soldiers fall to the ground.

Scene 8

The final preparations

The Grey Infantry march suddenly breaks off. Enter the Family to the accompaniment of the Psalm.
There is a distinctive air about the way they enter this time, quite different from that of all previous entrances. You can feel that they are arriving for the last time, and with a special purpose in mind. They begin to line up chairs downstage with remarkable

meticulousness and ceremony. Clearly some decisive preparations are under way. Even the most ordinary of their activities break up into scarcely perceptible units, stages, fleeting and fragmentary.

Each minutest motion appears to arise out of a lengthy process of inner struggle and resolution. They collect the chairs from all sides — a veritable propagation of chairs. Conscientiously, they line them up in one row close to the audience. Little by little, a vague pattern, a mysterious design begins to shine through it all.

Father-on-Leave, with his broken ruler, measures all that happens to come his way: a self-evidently useless activity.

It becomes increasingly clear that nothing can be kept within its prescribed boundaries any longer, in accordance with an acceptable set of values and proportions — things begin to unfold spontaneously, abruptly, headlong. Indeed, the room, so far keeping itself afloat pretty well, is suddenly going full speed towards its imminent epilogue.

Behind the row of chairs are naked dummies like condemned men, behind them a forest of crosses, still further off — the Army. Rifles stick up, with fixed bayonets. The Family in full force take their seats downstage. An air of anticipation hangs over them.

Suddenly the two Uncles rush out. Soon they are back dragging an enormous board along. They cleave their way through the solid *wall* of bodies, chairs, naked soldiers. They are quite ruthless. They scatter everything that lies in their path. The Priest collapses, the naked dummies, chairs and people go down after him.

However, right on their heels follow two soldiers with another enormous board. Menacingly, the two boards hover over the heads of the actors. Any moment these two heavy objects, dirty and spattered with mud, brought from God knows where, or for what

purpose, will crash onto the stage, smashing everything and everybody around.

Eventually the boards descend on to the forestage, where they are propped up somehow or other, or maybe the actors themselves will hold them. Everything totters. Confusion.

The massive sound of the Psalm imposes a religious dimension on it all.

Against the rising tension, the Family persist with their hoary arguments, resentments and retrospection, as if they had little time to lose. And yet over and beyond their gestures, which solemnly and crudely struggle to revive the ultimate geometry of the divine Leonardo, one can already glimpse the very thing, a first sign of *The Last Supper*.

Scene 9

The inevitable white table cloth.

And when an immaculately white, ceremonially starched *cloth* with sharp-ironed folds is being laid over the muddy, sand-and-lime coated boards, we have no doubt any longer that despite all the prior scandals, intrusions, undesirable guests, let alone iconographic ignorance, we shall indeed bear witness to *The Last Supper*.

Scene 10

The Last One . . .

The Psalm and *The Grey Infantry* begin to
merge. The naked corpses of soldiers
shamelessly press forward.
Evidently, the Army at the rear have grown
insubordinate; unregulated mechanisms turn
anarchic and destructive. Rising from the
ground, staggering and toppling over each
other, they struggle to hold aloft the
graveyard crosses, their own rifles, the
stripped bodies of those killed in action,
deluded, frenzied, they push everything to
the edge of the stage, dangerously close to
the audience — the wardrobe, the *table*, the
chairs, the *window*, the *bed* — a monstrous
pulp of wreckage.
Right in front of the audience, the *wardrobe*
is open both at the front and rear. The
soldiers pass through it, leaping blindly,
dancing to the rhythm of a devilish cabaret;
shameless, naked corpses of soldiers are
strewn on the ground.
The Priest lies among them, battered. The
repulsive Photographer's Widow sets her
lethal camera at the ready.
A volley.
The soldiers fall, swearing, screaming;
bodies and objects pile up, then freeze.
The participants of *The Last Supper* have
frozen as well, around the table, caught
in their emotive gesticulations . . . .

Scene 11

The Christmas Carol.

The Deportee-Busker comes up with his last concert. The carol can be heard. The Gospels' *Last Supper* overlapping with Christmas — on all the battle-fields that are crammed in this room from our childhood.

Scene 12

In the end everybody must leave.

The carol goes on.
Over this last Christmas table, an enormous cross looms and sways, held by one of the soldiers . . .
Slowly the Actors retreat from the stage, moving backwards, looking behind them, they vanish little by little . . .
The Priest remains on the ground.
The stage becomes empty, no people, no objects. Then, from the hall the Little Rabbi in his synagogue garments approaches the Priest, helps him up and leads him away.

I go up to the table. After very carefully folding the table-cloth, I stick it under my arm and go out.

Director's Notes

on Rehearsals

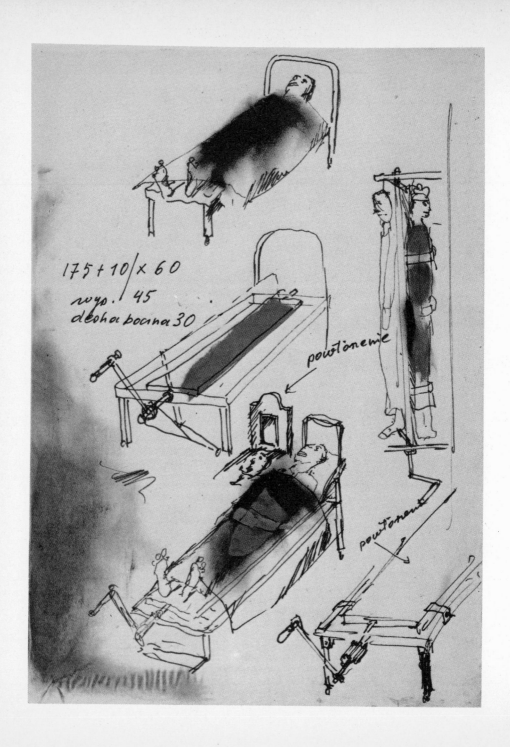

The Platoon as a Species of Humanity

. . . to focus on just one characteristic of THE PLATOON, the most fundamental, broaching this topic only after rejecting a whole gamut of traits which may be very striking but are hackneyed nevertheless: namely, the expressionist — as for instance the danger of life under fire, trenches, mud, more mud, open country, dirt, wounds, gangrene, amputations, death, skeletons, graves, crosses . . . the parodic, like sadistic sergeants, sclerotic colonels, generals as death's grim high priests; the patriotic, viz the allure of arms, cavalry charges, landscapes after battle, standards flapping in the wind of history, pantheons of glory and Unknown Soldiers . . . To renounce all these gimmicks, which have in any case lost all their impact, is to be left with a very limited field of reference, but one which seems to me to contain the metaphysical heart of the matter, and to offer the actor new possibilities: namely, that the PLATOON is a distinct SPECIES OF HUMANITY, cut off from us CIVILIAN SPECTATORS by a barrier. Crossing it is strictly forbidden, and in any case inconceivable like death itself.

N.B. The Lot of the Platoon and that of the Actor

. . . When I turned my mind to devising a new show, one which would constitute the next step after *Dead Class*, I set greatest store by finding a new model that the actors could make use of, enlarging their scope for action.

My *open sesame*, which transported me to strange heights of euphoria and set me off on a fresh scent, was the sudden excitement I felt at seeing a souvenir photograph of raw recruits apparently waiting to be sent to the front, grey, pitiful figures transfixed in the attitude of death, which had singled them out and dressed them in this horrific uniform.

THE PLATOON

Two deep-seated characteristics of the platoon mirrored the age-old stigmata borne by the actor: one was their IRREVOCABLE and FUNDAMENTAL DIFFERENCE (like the dead), their DIFFERENCE from us CIVILIAN — SPECTATORS, to such a degree that a barrier was erected that it was UNTHINKABLE to cross, as in a nightmare. And the other thing one was horrifyingly aware of, again a nightmare experience, was that this DIFFERENCE was manifested by beings of our own species, that WE are these ALIENS, the DEAD, that we are confronting our own image and we must MERGE WITH IT! An uncanny resemblance:

THE PLATOON (the individual soldier is a different thing) and THE ACTOR.

Etudes — Sketches of a Scenario

. . . I turn over in my mind ways in which I might create the right ambience and conditions for the PLATOON to be identified existentially with the ACTOR.
On stage we have a PLATOON, stuck in the corner of the ROOM.
Soldiers advancing upon us from the past, 'dead', stripped down, as it were, to a single grimace and a single moment, 'resurrected' (I shall have to find some stage motif to indicate this 'miracle') acting with a sort of lack of conviction, tangential to life and to memory.
Nothing mysterious, of course, about these symptoms, which simply express what it is to be a PLATOON.
But the ROOM also contains (in addition to the furtive PLATOON) CIVILIAN — ACTORS,
whose appearance, behaviour and mentality
are close to — blood-relations of — the SPECTATORS.
The SPECTATORS identify with the CIVILIAN — ACTORS
in the degree zero of expressivity,
and by means of this process discover within themselves little
by little
a similar if not identical state of being to that of the PLATOON THEY EXPERIENCE — ALL THOSE SENSATIONS AND FEELINGS which
arise on being confronted with oneself, stripped down to an
empty shell, a thing,
THE DEAD.
A tide is set in motion, and its ebb and flow discloses
always more clearly and unequivocally
THE FACE OF HUMANITY.
THE PLATOON — a particular genus of humanity —
thus constituting the MODEL of the actor.
As the action unfolds, so, gradually, they emerge for what they are.

The PLATOON scenes are
garish,
circus-like,
split-second,
quick as a flash,
like greased lightning,
at the double,
ragtime,
like an image of a brothel in hell,
all frenzied jerking —
not, for God's sake, a subject for edifying contemplation,
or moralizing —
which would really be most inappropriate in the Big Top of Death.

CONSCRIPTION
is a sort of funeral.
The recruiting officers are two gloomy CIVILIANS in black.
Like gravediggers.
Then a tiny barrier.
Behind which is the Naked One.
The officers measure him with a ruler.
From this side and that.
Up and down.
They stretch him out on the ground. Flat.
Pass judgement.
Bear him off like a corpse.
The prostitute beats the clappers like mad.

DRILL IN PUTTING TO DEATH INDIVIDUALS OF THE SAME SPECIES.
DRILL IN DYING BY NUMBERS

DRILL in subhuman levelling down.
Bestializing.
The way you feel in a crowd of men stripped naked.
Masochistic feeling of biological levelling down.
The violation of one's individuality.
Marching strictly in step, serried ranks, one — two, feet, hands, bodies, feet, feet, feet . . .
war's ritual dance,
coarse, barrack-room oaths
obscene press of bodies.

Numbering off — I am a cipher, a number . . .

Lining up — and lining up again, and again.

FALLING IN — the word of command, no sooner shouted than acted upon — the reflex absolutely instantaneous — however absurd the drill, however irrational, repeated over and over and over, endlessly.

As one man, they all perform the same movement.

Marching. Machine-like. Soulless.
And they know no other way.
Absurd. In the ROOM, among the furniture.
What a disgrace!
Surely they are mentally retarded. Arrested development.
Touched.

SEX AND DEATH

1978

Notes on the Platoon

The platoon is in the room.
Six or eight soldiers will do, wearing uniforms and carrying rifles,
all the colour of lead.
They appear to have stepped out of a souvenir photograph.
How they came to be in this room, no one can guess: it is like a dream.
Here they live some kind of secret life.
And here they will stay, living their lives without any regard for the tenants of this
ROOM. Right next to them.
No one pays them any attention. They are dumb.
This is how they will live out their lives, in holes and corners.
Gradually everyone gets used to their presence. But they remain alien. They are fearful at first,
timid, but as they begin to feel more at home and see how the land lies they start up their usual
exercises, manoeuvres, until even the room begins to look like a battlefield. . .

November 1979

Notes on the Platoon

Keep in mind the strange existential reality of THE PLATOON, and that special aura which emanates
from it.

ALIENATION

We feel similarly alienated from *the dead*, from the contagious, from the insane:
an acutely painful severance of every kind of CONTACT.
And other feelings follow from this: dread, loathing, menace
are expressed by:
a certain troubling and equivocal immobility,
dead faces,
mouths open as if to scream, are dumb,
the gait of a sleepwalker, as in obedience to the will of another, a solitary soldier sits motionless
with his gun, behind the wardrobe, in the corner, glimpsed in the vestibule, gazing with dead eyes
towards the room, a ghost . . .
in a dream,
like a corpse.
And this presence of theirs, obtrusive and overbearing, lacks any practical application.

Their similarity to *objects* is overwhelming.
You could walk past and not notice them, bump into them easily, knock them over or rearrange
them like furniture — like dead things.
They in turn advance towards the 'civilians' with unseeing eyes,
Two *alien* species that can never make contact,
so remote are they from each other, so tragically and evidently estranged.
The platoon MARCHES.
Its marching is not natural
but artificial
circus-like
embarrassing.
(Marching as such does not fully describe this bizarre style of movement.
You have to imagine someone who, in the midst of a hurrying crowd, in a busy street, struts on rigid
legs, waves his arms, stiff-necked, eyes staring vacantly.)

The biological condition:

men
in serried ranks
pressed up against one another
bodies squeezed against bodies
legs intertwined with legs
hands with hands
heads with heads
a herd
all belonging to the same Species.
no need for privacy
no shame
almost naked . . .

December 1979

Notes on the Platoon

The language of the Huns.
The Roman officers related that Atilla, addressing his troops before battle, barked like a DOG.

THE PLATOON has come to stay. They will continue to inhabit the room.
They have really settled in, they feel at home here.
They drill in this little room, fall in, manoeuvre, and in the event of war, would doubtless
engage the enemy here. But you have to think of all this taking place on the margins of life, going

unremarked, unnoticed, in some sense impotent and sneaky.
Just like *the dead*, after all,
they do not enter into any living association with the 'live' tenants of the ROOM.
They slip into this room
as if in a *dream*
like those long dead.
The house of childhood is a house of the *dead*,
it must have something of the cemetery about it.
(I have been told that deep in the interior of Mexico there is a custom of keeping the dead in the house, in niches hewn in the rock.
At All Souls they collect their dead and seat them at the table, dried out, shrivelled up, just bones and sinews. . . .)

December 1979

Notes on the Platoon

Taken at Rehearsal sometime in December

Recruiting
may be treated as a *children's game*. Playing at recruits.
The Two Uncles are grownups, of course. It is evident that they are even strangely advanced in years (perhaps as a consequence of sickness, poverty, or life's vicissitudes) — yet at the same time they are miserable specimens who have not succeeded in reaching the practical stage of maturity required by the physical age of any right-thinking person. They lack sobriety and gravity, as if arrested in their development, and have proved unwilling to leave the happy land of childhood and the realm of imagination unconstrained by rationality. Perhaps they will be judged to be mentally defective and in the heat of their performance seen as possessed, raving mad.
Thus they can play out their game, like children playing with toys, with great success. And this should be the principle underlying the production.
The Uncles strip one of the raw recruits stark naked, making it quite clear that they are fully-fledged members of the recruiting party.
They shove the naked man out of the door. They sit down in the armchairs.
They wait.
They say 'next'.
It looks as if they want to give the impression that there are a large number of recruits, that they have been terribly busy. This single recruit must therefore stand in for a large number of others.

Notes on the Platoon

The platoon
Abject tenants of the ROOM!
They gradually settle in.
Soon they begin their drill
an assault
they shout
crawl forward
run full tilt across the stage
take cover behind furniture. . . .
fall in. . . .
But this rehearsal does not seem to me a success. I decide to bring them to a halt.
A platform is made in the workshop, a much more powerful effect with a greater visual 'immediacy': the soldiers are placed on a moving platform (a sort of child's push-cart) and march on the spot. I wonder whether to keep this platform as a regular feature of their activities.
And by so doing construct a 'matrix' (like the benches in *Dead Class*), with an inevitable effect on their style of performance, their movements, their being: imposing a structure upon them.

December 1979

Notes on the Platoon

Keeping in mind that
THE PLATOON
is *dead*
has shed both its blood and its memory
in some obscure cataclysm
as a direct consequence of
repetition
(the photograph)
all that is left of them is a piece of paper,
the attitude struck,
shreds of life, inert clichés.

And should you attempt to revive some fragment of their life (only on the stage, of course) they will cry out in the language of the barrack room, having lost for ever their faculties of discourse and memory — they will jerk and twitch, lunge viciously, charge, kill, start off in any direction, fight to the death with who knows whom, collapse and die.

January 1980

Scenes with the Platoon

At Rehearsal, March 31, 1980

As usual, the beginning is chaotic.
Actors wandering around the stage, singly or in groups, some foolish remarks. I was simply anxious that they should not start 'playing their part', get carried away, that they should be themselves, not public performers: in case I am suddenly struck by an idea, an image or a situation catches my attention. Something is beginning to take shape. . . .

Some metal clasps have been prepared for the rehearsal; I use these, together with padlocks, to fasten together the soldiers, who are standing sentry in pairs. They form a British Square. One of them thrusts his hand vigorously into the air. The others, responding abruptly to this gesture, copy it, but, as it were, reluctantly: clumsily, feebly, grotesquely. Facial expressions have to convey a range of different attitudes: bewilderment, flinching from a blow, stress, terror, the urge to run for it, haste, panic, the admission of defeat at the hopeless effort of not breaking ranks.
The Square is initially absolutely regular, uniform, in response to a word of command coming from God knows where — but gradually it becomes a jumble of threshing arms, legs, torsoes and twisted faces. This collective organism looks like some kind of nightmarish machine the moving parts of which are
people
deprived of their free will,
their individual freedom violated,
tortured,
dehumanized.
We see before our eyes a reified abstract of that special product of the artificial selection of the Human Species known as: THE PLATOON.

Another group, a different species, constitutes the civilians.
The tenants of the room.
My Family.
Uncle Karol, Auntie Józka, Uncle Olek, Grandma. . . .
They are already old friends of ours. Auntie Mańka has dressed up as Himmler again. The cap of familiar cut: the long, baggy, dirty raincoat — her face hidden by the huge turned-up collar — on her feet are ugly children's boots. Grey all over, including her face — and somehow pathetic, like a child, in her menacing uniform.

The Family are completely at a loss in the face of Mad Mańka's ideas.
She struts like a doll.
The members of the family keep repeating snatches of their usual banal conversations — but all higgledy-piggledy.
They sit down at the table.
The TABLECLOTH also keeps them together, since they fasten it at their throats with belts and braces — like a napkin at lunch.
But the tablecloth is an enormous military field map.
The sort you find in HQ.
Genuine and gigantic.
It speaks of war. Without equivocation.
There you have it: it is the *thing* that performs, communicates,
represents.
The actors remain on its margins.

Another variant of THE PLATOON.

So these are the soldiers:
their existence in this show as in this ROOM
was clearly defined as early as the first scene:
they belong to the world of *repetition*, the outcome of practices which I would describe as unclean,
something that happens in the dark and dubious
recesses and outbuildings of life.
They are a replica therefore fraudulent, the living dead from birth.
Denuded of a past, or any subsequent life.
They have forgotten everything. They have settled for a single moment of life.
They live on the margins of life.

March 31, 1980

Family Portrait or For Ever and Ever Amen

Rehearsal February 2, 1980, Thursday, the same theme continued on April 3, 1980

In a corner
behind the wardrobe
we put up the cross.

There it looks very strange indeed.
It makes its presence felt in the ROOM,
not the proper place for it (like a church
or a cemetery).

When it was set up in the centre of the stage as a 'signifier', the crucifix was not truly in a room, although
surrounded by walls and furniture,
this was simply the stage, a place where anything that is is explicable. The cross could have been the one on Golgotha, or one in a cathedral, a chapel, a graveyard. The point of the show is to continuously eliminate the notion of the STAGE, while focusing upon the existence of the ROOM. Indeed, the room, rather than existing on the stage,
must strive to become a genuine room, existent in itself.

Everything that happens in the room is to
happen in this very room and no other,
whether it be the Crucifixion, the Last Supper,
the military manoeuvres, war, or the Last Judgement.

IN THE ROOM (behind the wardrobe, in a corner) the cross loses much of its symbolism,
becoming a concrete thing.
After all, this is some kind of presbytery, as is evident from the presence of the priest,
and the crucifix may have been moved from the church, say, for renovation, and for the time being left in the corner.
We may even act it out thus: one of the tenants
brings in the crucifix in an 'ordinary' manner.
The Priest will examine it. Having found it needs
no repairs he will put it aside in the corner.
The scene may smack of naturalism, yet it will help to play down the pathos of the situation and of the object itself, already sufficiently laden with symbolism.
By becoming material and tangible, thanks to this down-to-earth treatment,
the cross will look even more disturbing and uncanny, when the right moment comes.

Next, we open the wardrobe (the door at the front),
Then the opposite door at the rear (the wardrobe is somewhat strange: it opens from both sides).

Now, looking through the wardrobe we can see the middle distance: the corner of the room with the crucifix.
As if we were looking into a different space, onto another stage.
A stage within a stage.
The wardrobe turns into the wings.
Yet at the same time, all this is quite obviously a blatant conjuring trick.
A good idea, this one.
Let's hold on to it.

When he enters the wardrobe, the Priest looks ridiculous. And when he emerges on the other side and stops before the cross, he suddenly finds himself in a different, unreal, space. And when he then raises his head towards the cross, as if posing for a picture,
adopting, as I put it, the 'eternity' pose,
he is already on the other side of death.

Uncle Karol, bored, is looking out of the window.

Suddenly, he catches sight of someone he knows.
He opens the window. Leaning out with a smile,
he takes off his hat with a flamboyant gesture to say 'hello'.
And so he too remains
fixed for 'eternity'.

Adaś, possibly for the first time, has a pair of long trousers on, and a high white starched collar with a black tie,
just like the Uncles wear.
He brings a chair in, puts it in the centre of the stage, and sits down,
crossing his legs (again in the style of the Uncles).
He turns his head in profile; apparently Fate approves this pose as the height of perfection, and, turning the left cheek, he stays smiling eternally at
something beyond our ken.

Grandma Katarzyna stares horrified at the dead priest who has turned rigid 'in the beyond' — her hand, with its otiose bedpan, hanging down limply.
With her other hand on the door-knob, she directs her gaze towards her brother
— as if to set her mind at rest about something — and in this manner, hovering by the door, she freezes for eternity.

Father decides once and for all to leave the house, which he has come to hate.
He lingers in the hall with his suitcase and rifle and lets off a volley of barrack-room oaths. He glances round the room for the last time. The moment must seem to him a very special one, for he takes off his shako and holds it at his side, like a real soldier,
and so, standing in the hall, bare-headed, a curse dying on his lips, he remains.

Mother Helka roams through the House of the Dead in her wedding veil, trying to find someone who could help her grasp the sole gesture that lingers from the past in her wretched bruised mind: the matrimonial gesture of the binding of the hands with the priest's stole — she clutches hold of the stole as she walks. But all of them now are dead, except for
Uncle Olek,
whom Uncle Karol deserted. To him he turns
crying in despair
'and me, what about me?'
But Uncle Karol is past hearing,
entirely absorbed in eternally raising his hat.
Crazed Mother Helka takes his hand,
pulls it towards her, binds it with her stole,
she staggers
the same as before,
Uncle Olek holds her by the waist
the same as she was held by Father,
yet doing it mechanically
as if feeling constrained
he keeps shouting in the direction of Uncle Karol

'and me? what about me?'
as if asking him for help.
Mother:
'and now I was being dragged along,
I was being dragged along.'

Uncle Olek,
disconsolate,
drags her along
against his will —

and in this moment
in this pose
they are caught
by the ruthless Photographer — Death.

Auntie Józka
and Auntie Mańka
sit at the table
stupefied.
They are left by themselves, alone,
each staring towards her husband.
Auntie Mańka shouts:
'Karol, Karol'.
Auntie Józka:
'Olek, Olek' . . .
Auntie Mańka:
'He was always chasing a bit of skirt'
Auntie Józka:
'Leave Helka alone,
you old ruffian.'
These two miserable specimens
go limp at the table
and their faces retain their expressions of stupefaction
for ever.

The Room and the Anteroom
An analysis of these Concepts

February 29, 1980

These general, somewhat metaphysical reflections relate to my earlier remark that the function of things happening *outside*, behind the door, in the hall (that is on the periphery) had not been properly emphasized.

Hence this analysis of these concepts, with a view to putting things right today. Let's try to determine the overall scheme of the production, supposing this can be done at all.

It is difficult to define
the spatial dimensions of memory.
THE ROOM is the one where I spent my childhood.
A Dead Room
inhabited by the Dead.
I keep setting up
the house, which is gone:
it dies over and over
together with the tenants
who are my family.
They are endlessly busy
doing the same things
over and over, as if
their movements were preserved
on a negative, for ever and ever.
They will carry on in this wise
until you are sick and tired of them
clinging to one pose,
a single twist of the face,
trapped in their trivial doings,
glued to basic movements,
movements without expression,
ghastly, precise,
dogged, bluntly emphatic,
the trivial actions that fill our lives.
In the meantime
BEHIND THE DOOR, behind the façade of the ROOM,
the domain of the HORRID GROWN-UPS, or shall we say,
their remains,
things are clearly happening that will fill the Spectator with a number of distinct impressions.

1. That these weird goings-on must be a game
played by a group of CHILDREN.
That they are children, you will gather
from the *constriction of the space*: children are known
to love tiny spaces,
in which to hide from the GROWN-UPS,
such *places* as:
nooks and corners,
behind-the-wardrobe,
in-the-attic,
under-the-landing,
behind-the-door;
children know full well that these Regions of the Lowest Order
belong to the realm of the imagination,
where you may uncover the Mystery of Life and the Real.
That they are children is borne out by
the *mimicry* of their faces, sullenly pensive and alert —
in marked contrast to their *fidgety* movements,
haphazard actions, their *conventionality*.

2. It will also occur to the spectator
that these strange actions (the strangeness of life:
we do not yet know for sure what sort of actions they are)
have been *dismissed* to the outskirts of the ROOM,
in a *Region of the Lowest Order*,
from which grown-ups stay away,
like, for instance, an attic,
where you throw old junk, already
half-belonging to the scrap-heap, where things are left to die.

3. You will have yet another impression:
that the zone of wonders and wondrous acts
can *never be compatible* with the adult way of thinking
and its joyless materialism.
(This will be gleaned from the way they behave
stealthily   mimicry
                — conspiracy —
                typical gesticulation
hurriedly   as if apprehensive that their doings will be
                exposed and forbidden, or get them into trouble.)

4. And you will indulge in certain consequent reflections:
that this is the *world of childhood*,
a realm forlorn,
forgotten
(by the awful grown-ups)

assassinated
abandoned to *Contempt*.
Only when he has fallen for these impressions
will the spectator feel
that in the lost world of childhood —
shrouded in slippery memories and pure
invention
in the most god-forsaken region
we may run to earth the lost myth of the Gospels —
— to me, a work of Pure Poetry —
and a forgotten stage of feeling:
human tears.

Some Mistakes and some Errors of Judgement

The turmoil that bursts out of the hall
— the door being flung open again and again
— the cross, the ladder, the bits of scaffolding, the swirling bodies —
all of this pointed unmistakeably to some dramatic
activity on the other side, maybe much
more important than the travails
this side of the DOOR.

This strange, unsettling scurrying to and fro might perhaps make sense in terms of its very
inscrutability, its plasticity.
So fascinating was this scene in its own right, as an image, that its meaning, let's say,
had grown obscure even to me.

A pure image, a picture, the influence of the Uffizi on me, was it?

When it comes down to it, the relationship between the ROOM
where life goes on, with its impossible yet sanctioned vacuity,
and the PLACE OF WRETCHEDNESS (BEHIND THE DOOR) nursing
the memories of those Departed Days
will make sense of the whole show.
So let us keep clearly in mind
what it means to be pushed aside
to be poor and wretched
to squat in holes and corners; let us acknowledge
the outlawed
        prohibited

persecuted
way of being.
All the activities BEHIND THE DOOR must therefore be purged of the picturesque. They are to become *acts*, with a distinct aim and motive.

The Rehearsal: a Record

The dead priest soaks his feet in a basin
telling his beads.
A racket behind the door:
The percussion of hammer-blows, a saw, people running.
THE PRIEST
at the end of his tether, rushes to the door, opens it.
The racket stops abruptly.
The CHILDREN scurry off like cockroaches.
In the hollow of the hall —
'those things', abandoned.
The priest goes back to where he was.
Reassured.
Silence reigns for a while.
But not for long.
Again: a racket of hammering, sawing, running feet.
UNCLE KAROL
for all his preoccupation with his headache
decides at last to step in, goes up to the door,
and opens it abruptly.
Behind the door — panic.
Silence falls:
nobody is there.
Uncle Karol closes the door
and sits down at the table as before,
giving himself up to his headache.

We have peace and quiet for the time being.

There they go again:
noises, shouts, hammering, sawing.
FATHER-ON-LEAVE
immersed in the entrails of his suitcase
and rifle, traverses the floor
in his military manner. He flings open the door

seizing a splendid opportunity to throw in loud and
sordid barrack-room curses.
He closes the door. Unable to calm down.

On the other side the CHILDREN must have got used to it all, for the racket bursts out afresh with
redoubled force.

This time it is Auntie Mańka's turn. Disguised as Himmler, a sordid strutting effigy, she enters the
hall.
Incomprehensible shouting, muffled commands.
You cannot tell what has happened.
Auntie Mańka-Himmler strides back into the room.
The CHILDREN following grotesquely behind her (or to be precise, the soldiers, who have just
donned priestly birettas.)
The lodgers round up the CHILDREN and begin to thrash them. The beating of children begins to
take on nightmarish proportions.
The CHILDREN slip out of the room, yet still for some time the lodgers continue to mete out
shadowy punishments in empty, pointless gestures.

A Correction of the Correction

Monday, March 3, 1980

Looking afresh over the notes from the last rehearsal,
I am disappointed.
These attempts to enlighten the spectator, *whether he likes it or not*, seem naive to me. That on this
side we have the GROWN-UPS, on the other the CHILDREN,
that the children are horrid,
that they enjoy pestering the busy boring grown-ups,
that they are kicked out of the ROOM because their way of life is alien to the adults.
ostracized,
and then punished —
all this is simplistic, illustrative, literal, just a genre
painting of Family Life.
First of all, we do not owe the Spectator extra information.
Something must remain *unspoken*;
reality, after all, is not merely the sum of its parts.

These CHILDREN — outcasts of the entrance hall —
are frightfully mature and tragic.
The GROWN-UPS in the ROOM, wrapped in their petty problems, behave like children.

Their odd games must be made *impenetrable*,

allowing *no bridge*, no fusion
with the affairs filling the room.
Children peeping shyly into the room
(in order to find out whether the GROWN-UPS are really and truly busy) — timid faces turned towards the centre of the room, and of course the audience,
are not what is wanted.
Scrap all this.

Apartness

Freezing still
as if posing for a photograph 'facing eternity'.
This facing of eternity is frightening.
There is a chill of death about it.
Ghostly.
Ghastly stillness.
Outlandishness
As in dreams.
A dream. The unreality
and Mysteriousness
that always hangs over children's games.
Impossible to say what they are up to.
Enigmatic movements, top-secret labours.

Vacuity

Now and again
when the door opens
the hall gapes hollow.
(God forbid we ever again have the children scurry off as the door opens. It is naive.)
The utter emptiness of the hall casts doubt upon its previous state (being filled with strangely energetic people.) Only towards the end does the cause of all this intriguing animation emerge: THE CROSS.

Scene: Adaś Departs for the Front

Rehearsal March 28, 1980 Friday

This scene was devised on March 13 and 14, but revised in the following fashion:

The Family is huddled around the table: Uncle Karol, Mad Mańka, Uncle Olek and Auntie Józka.
Their manner of sitting is unusual.
They look as if they were organically one with the table.
As if they were adrift on a stormy sea and the table was the last plank left to cling to.
The scene must convey the idea that some disaster has occurred. They hang on convulsively, shouting as if to drown out the roar of the ocean, God knows why, or who they are shouting to, they are terror-stricken, but their terror is inexplicable and has no connection with what they are talking about. It is the terror of being cut off from the contents of their own utterance. They are under the influence of Adaś's departure for the front. Adaś is missing. He appears later — a lot later.
It may be that we are witnessing a time-shift, since despite the fact that the Family is sitting, as before, at the table, their cries of *Adaś, Adaś get a move on*, directed at Adaś who is on the point of leaving for the front, grow fainter and fainter and seem to fade into the distance. . .
The old Priest, dead already long since, first picks up the army knapsack and rifle and puts them next to the little grave (a mound of yellow mud with a wretched little cross), dug in this childhood room — and then lifts Adaś in his arms, much as he lifted him once before from the cross, with the same gesture.
Slowly and carefully the Priest lowers the body to the earth.
But this frame evidently comes at a later point in time, when Adaś will lie on the shrapnel-scarred ground, dead.
This is how the sequence looks in the earlier rehearsal. But this time it will undergo substantial revision.
Despite the fact that this time-warp produced a vivid impression on all of us (initially Adaś was going to be placed 'alive' among the other recruits in the wagon), this 'entombment' struck me today as over-sentimental and 'patriotic'. These emotions had to be raised to a higher pitch, by means of shattering this 'graveside idyll' with a good strong dose of the Big Top, even of sacrilege.
Before the rehearsal, I looked over my earliest drawings, from the period when I first began to think about my new show. One of them was a sketch of a cross on primitive wheels. Christ, wearing jacket and trousers, pushed it along, walking alongside it. And this, precisely, was the Priest, returning after putting down Adaś's belongings, his knapsack and his rifle.
He is making his way back.
With a cross (his cross from Scene One).
The cross, leaning to one side, is pushed on a flimsy metal contraption fitted out with wheels.
The Priest pushes the cross as if it were a bicycle. On the cross (and on the bicycle) Adaś is spreadeagled.
We have stripped our earlier conception of all its sentimental pathos, its false representationalism.
The Priest has at once become just an actor performing his shameless and exhibitionistic trade. The road to tragic art as well as to pathos lies altogether elsewhere. To truth also.
As if on a railway station platform, the Exiled Violinist comes into view. The violinist has no violin. He has only the case left, and in this a hurdy-gurdy is concealed. He turns the crank with a sense of shame, suffering inwardly.
The carol from the Chopin *Scherzo* emerges, as expected, from the grotesquely misshapen violin case.
Another Big Top trick, designed to replace pathos by pure emotion. Not until this moment does the Priest appear with his mechanized cross and with Adaś.

The Priest carefully takes down the body of Adaś from the cross and lays it on the ground.
The doors at the back move aside.
A cattle truck.
The kind of truck they once used to transport conscripts to the front.
It is packed full of them.
This Dantesque vision is all the more frightening for being dumb and frozen:
the recruits are motionless, like rats caught in the fatal trap of 'illusions'.
shamelessly posed for their nightmarish photograph.
Into this seething
dumb
hell of debauchery
the old priest flings
the body of the dead Adaś.
Then, as if mechanically, from deep-seated habit, he casts earth on him as on a freshly-dug grave.
He does this with a movement both thorough and devout.
The Family runs along the platform.

The Rehearsal of February 2, 1980. A few General Reflections

Glancing over the earliest of these notes, I was taken back to the days when my conception of a new production was still waiting to be born. I realized how far these rehearsals have carried me from the time, which now seems as innocent as childhood, when a new land first swam into my ken. I understood the extent to which what was once sharply focused can become blurred.

An actor's rehearsals, which are essentially active, possess all those elemental qualities without which no creativity is possible. And yet this process has its own kinds of dangers: it can easily lose a sense of *direction*.

In the pre-history of this production, in the happy era when one was still free from the burden of practicalities, one could wander through the unpopulated regions of the imagination. In that ideal world of mine, certain transvaluations, transformations, and shifts occurred, which struck me as forcibly as if they had been rearrangements of the furniture in my own *room*.

I had always recoiled from the word Spiritualism.

Perhaps I had need of the reasoning faculty as a gland that stimulates in me a passion for the radical avant-garde, or was it simply as a shield against the absurdity of our world and the muddle of postwar culture? Be this as it may, I took strength from rationality in many adverse circumstances.

Yet the world is evidently more complicated than we suppose it to be. Indeed, it is precisely in the realm of Reason that the rot has set in.

Cracks and gaps are showing
all around the absolute wholeness
Reason was once claimed to be,
and the consequences prove fatal.

As in life so in art.
But above all in art.
Thus I find myself going back to the early days when, on my long solitary walks, I learned Maeterlinck's *Lesson* by heart. For at that age one can learn everything *by heart*.

Spiritualism and spirituality

(Obviously, my subject is still art. As to life, let's leave it on one side. Life is a personal matter, it must not be made into a pretext for art — at least, not while we are still among the living.)

Thinking over the new production, I saw the idea of spiritualism as offering a challenge, to the extent that it at once evoked associations with the Gospel, as if that might offer the only suitable means of expression.

What a splendid body of myth, the Gospel, and how close it is to Pure Art! The Gospel nourished our culture, and consequently the way we lived our lives for centuries, renewing itself constantly in each new era, only to be thrust rudely aside, in our century, to the margins of this civilization, with its sacred Technology, Mass-Consumption, and Politics. Not all is lost, however.

To be marginalized does not necessarily spell decline and humiliation. In my personal vocabulary there is a term: the Realm of the Lowest Order.
By which I mean a terrain reserved (illicitly) for Art.
That is, for the supreme human values.
The periphery holds pride of place in that realm.
The myth of the Gospel bursts its bounds in the most unlikely places,
indeed where else but at the periphery?
Or to put it in terms of art and poetry, in some wretched back-yard, or a gloomy corner, where our secret hopes lie buried together with our imagination, our threatened humanity, our sense of self.
Only in places like those, it seems, is salvation to be found.

The Scene of The Last Supper

March 12, 1980

The Scene of The Last Supper must take place BEHIND THE DOOR, secretively. In a CORNER as is generally the case with CHILDREN'S GAMES and their secret codes which the grown-ups don't understand. It needs to look pathetic and inadequate.
The door to the ROOM is open.
The whole family takes part in The Last Supper:
Uncle Karol, Uncle Olek, Auntie Mańka, Auntie Józka, Grandma and Adaś.

The scene of the *Crucifixion* is set up and acted out by the soldiers who, after changing their clothes and putting on priests' birettas, have regressed to childhood. The way I see it, these 'gospel' games played by children on the quiet, away from the grown-ups who won't interrupt them, should gradually begin to make an impact on the 'official' stage and catch the imagination of the grown-ups.

The 'gospel' scenes are not really acted by children.
This would be naively literal,
It is simply that the space BEHIND THE DOOR, the secret place of the imagination, conjures up a special aura, it is under a spell, and brings about profound changes in the actors, transforming them into children.
It is, as it were, another dimension of space, that of the imagination.
The thing is to discover this OTHER SPACE.
This will be accomplished as it is set down,
'on the quiet'
in other words, hastily,
in trepidation
ineffectually, sort of,
and — of course — without any practical results,
like something wretched
trashy
contemptible
unworthy of notice —
lacking any appropriate expression, which at least might have made it PLAUSIBLE*
in terms of ACTUAL FACT —
but in response to some ENIGMATIC CODE.
This transformation need not start from any given image presented to the imagination — the more so, since these are 'grown-up' actors — tenants of the ROOM — but rather from preparatory scenarios having the character of PLOT, CONSPIRACY, or SUBTERFUGE (maybe even of RECOLLECTION).

The rear walls are pushed back. The door remains open. The whole of the antechamber 'box' is visible.
The table is inclined diagonally towards the front of stage.
Cramped and crowded round the table is the family, tenants of the ROOM.
Their movements are exaggerated, convulsive.
They are squabbling about the will.
The actors, for once, may improvise.
On the floor of the ROOM lies the Priest (the Dummy).

*N.B. It is well known that grown-ups, who accept only ACTUAL FACT and cannot stand mystification, will warmly welcome art which passes itself off as the concrete reality with which it identifies.

This family scene, already scandalous enough, is soon to be transformed into 'The Last Supper'.
Composed in such a way that it looks as though a slide of Leonardo's well-known painting has been superimposed on it.
In view of the fact that the negative hero of this scene is Judas, I call to mind the Rabbi from Wielopole.
The Rabbi is indispensible. It is highly possible that he will play a vital part later on.
Auntie Mańka — the lunatic — must dress up as the Rabbi.
(The character of the Rabbi is created *extempore**, on the stage; a skull-cap, sidelocks, white shawl with black stripes, some make-up, and the Rabbi is already sitting there among the family — who are scandalized by this transformation.
They shout: *Mańka, what do you mean by it, how dare you.* . .
The Mańka/Rabbi character sings the *Rebecca* chant.
Not as some imposing psalm, but — in keeping with the tradition of the Cricot theatre — a vulgar song from a dubious sort of cabaret.
The squabbling about the will goes on (this can be written in Polish, German, and some technical jargon from Yiddish.)

The actors crushed together in the ANTECHAMBER squeeze through the door, jumbled together with the table and chairs.
Now they are in the ROOM.
Two leaves are drawn out to make the table bigger.
Now it is as long as in Leonardo da Vinci's picture.
Gradually the scene of the squabble about the will is transformed into the scene of 'The Last Supper'. The actors shout and wave their arms. A psalm is heard. It gets louder and louder and then is suddenly cut off.

At the same moment all movement stops, and the voice of a single actor is cut off. He freezes in an attitude taken from Leonardo's picture, and all the others follow suit. Finally the Priest, seated in the middle, opens his arms in the familiar gesture. And so, with devilish precision, an image forms amid the geometry of shoulders, outstretched hands, faces, taut bodies, all reacting to one single utterance: 'one of you will betray me'.

*N.B. The dressing-up might be made more spontaneous if I, for instance, were to dress up Auntie Mańka on the stage.

A later note, March 17

The Deportee-Violinist

Wednesday, March 12, 1980

Working out the details of UNCLE STAŚ' role. Uncle Staś returned in 1921 from Russian captivity somewhere in far-away Tashkent. He was an artist who painted pictures which were very fine indeed; and he played the violin. He came back covered with lice, and with a Russian wife. An Austrian officer turned Russian prisoner, he had found his way, after the war ended, to a transport of released soldiers.

I am quite sure he had nothing of the allure of those Siberian deportees who, following a series of national catastrophes and lamentations, would inhabit our martyrological iconography, only to become reunited, at the end of their lives, with their country and families.

And yet because, in this show, time is foreshortened, the archetypal hero of national lamentation has suddenly superimposed himself on our Uncle. So he is a deportee, and a violinist as well. However, since all our characters actually issue from a *Rental Service* of doubtful reputation, the violinist-deportee turns out to be an ordinary vagrant busker. His wretched violin case, imbued with the promise of a grand concert, turns out to be a crude hurdy-gurdy, resting, to make it worse, on an invalid's crutch, and ineptly concealing a crank with which to wind the mechanism.

Well, this ghastly apparition is more than a concept, it also helps to solve a few consequent formal problems.

The risky emotive make-believe of a *patriotic hero in romantic costume*
is *demystified*, he becomes
a dubious type of second-rate comedian from suburban theatricals.
A tragic past of captivity and war is reflected
in this distorting mirror, flashing its ghastly smile —
a smile capable of dislodging exhausted theatrical ritual with all its
representationalism,
posturing,
unbearable illustrative devices —
the bane of all our theatres,
where the pathos of history
or the nation,
are taken on board
with such terribly apparent seriousness.
Precisely this Big Top glitter
makes it possible for us
to catch a glimpse, be it only a glimpse,
of the *core of the Real*,
or to be fair, its residue.

One thing more, and I have finished:
the sound of the carol
from Chopin's scherzo,

barbarously mutilated
(orgues de Barbari!)
by this gross instrument
puts us in touch
with the unhackneyed
pure (!)
essence
of all the Christmas Eves
of our childhood.

A note: After the rehearsal, in which the deportee-violinist began to function as a framing device
for other events, I felt that he ought to reappear as a lone figure in the finale, or rather the sort of
'non-finale', of the show.

The Rabbi's Song — a Continuation of The Last Supper

Rehearsal, Thursday and Friday March 3 and 4

The family row about the will goes on in the antechamber.
The corpse-Priest (a wax dummy) lies in the ROOM, on the floor.
The actor (live) stands over these dead remains.
The Priest is 'doubled' by recollection — REPETITION.
This image is full of meaning. It is a kind of set piece that must
linger in the mind's eye and focus attention on its significance.
In it you will find the basic idea of the whole show.
Repetition.
The impotence of ILLUSION (as far as life is concerned).
Soldiers, like a photograph.
Dead.
Father sits on the ground in the front row with crossed legs
(this is always the case in souvenir photographs).
Every so often a thought strikes him and distracts his attention.
There is a ferment in his mind.
He changes the position of a leg.
The compassionate priest assists him in this (as it were) 'embrionic'
movement. He helps him up (just as he was helped up in the first scene, the wedding).
The Father stands up,
and at once begins
to curse
and march.
The Mother
(still wearing her bridal veil)

walks straight towards him.
The Priest watches this encounter,
abortive as ever,
with a look of indulgence and sadness.
The family, all on top of one another
in the antechamber
round the table
leave off quarrelling about the will
and start on the *funeral*.

They stand over the waxwork corpse.
Cover him with a black shroud, with great solicitude.
Looks of anguish on their faces.
The solemn words of the Mass for the Dead.
From time to time one of them cannot stand the strain, and blurts out something about the will and all the grounds for dispute.
And the artificial ceremony drags on.
While suddenly
as if he had just materialized from the wings
like a jack-in-the-box
the wretched Rabbi pops up
and dances over the body of the Priest
singing his miserable *Rebecca*.
The Family are scandalized, take flight, and scatter in all directions.
The rabbi sings and wrings his hands in despair —
But the soldiers have already had enough of this. They start up abruptly and shoulder their rifles, all taking aim simultaneously with the speed of light — like a firing squad.
A volley rings out.
The poor Rabbi falls to the ground.
This frame will be re-used very much later.

Repetition.
The Rabbi gets up,
Again he sings, and dances, undeterred.
A volley.
He falls . . .

The Rabbi's Song (A Fragment)

March 14, 1980

THE FAMILY SQUABBLE about the will goes on in the ANTECHAMBER.
On the floor of the ROOM lies the corpse of the PRIEST.
The corpse is a wax dummy — a mannequin.
However, the PRIEST who stands over the corpse — a live actor — constitutes a RECOLLECTION or REPETITION.
As a living, performing actor he possesses all the necessary skills to play out all the consequences of the arbitrary act of REITERATION.
This image (or cinematic frame) is of the utmost significance. Somehow it must be 'held', reinforced, given special emphasis.
In this image resides the essence of the show and of my theatre.
Repetition.
The life-impotence of ILLUSION.
Soldiers like a snapshot.
On this occasion they are positioned downstage,
in the right-hand corner.
Father, legs crossed, sits on the ground, in the front row,
(this is always the way in family photographs).
From time to time something 'comes over him' or 'strikes' him.
Something working entirely from within.
He moves his leg.
The compassionate priest helps him to make one of these abortive movements.
He gives him a helping hand (as he helped him up in the first scene — before the wedding).
Father gets up,
and at once begins
swearing
marching.
Mother
(still wearing her bridal veil)
goes to meet him.
The priest watches their
continually frustrated
encounter
with melancholy forebearance.

The family, in serried ranks
around the table
in the antechamber
change the subject of their squabbling
from the will

to the funeral.

The dear departed dummy
is carefully draped in black canvas.
Doleful miens.
Solemn prayers for the dead.
The hollow charade is taking its course
when suddenly
like a marionette
launched from out of the wings
enter the wretched Rabbi
dancing and singing
over the Priest's body
his miserable chant.
The outraged family scatters, taking flight. The Rabbi sings and wrings his hands in despair.
But the soldiers have already had enough of this. They rise suddenly and
shouldering their rifles, they take aim
Like a firing squad.
A volley of shots.
The poor Rabbi drops to the ground.
This frame should come very much later.

Re-run.
The Rabbi gets up.
Again he sings, dances, undeterred.
A volley of shots.
He falls. . .

The Scene of The Last Supper

April 2, 1980

The preceding version of 'The Last Supper' looks to me, on second thoughts, somewhat one-dimensional and flat. Some changes are essential — the images need a violent shake-up, their interaction should be more powerful, the superimposition of the FRAMES more striking.

The SOLDIERS have a ghastly look: a regiment of living corpses, confined to the corner, disgusting, like a pile of squirming maggots.

The movements of the FAMILY resemble a stampede, a panic-stricken evacuation in time of war.

And then the metamorphosis of Auntie Mańka — from a lunatic into the nightmarish puppet-figure of a Nazi general.

THE CIRCUS AT THE END OF TIME

A march-past of CRIPPLES AND CORPSES, soldiers mixed up with NAKED BODIES and GRAVEYARD CROSSES.

The NURSE with a corpse in her pram.

The return of Uncle Stasio — the Siberian exile, a mixture of HAWKER and BEGGAR, of CONJURER from the BIG TOP and PHONEY FIDDLE VIRTUOSO, with sham fiddle-cum-hurdy-gurdy.

The long table for the Last Supper is covered with a FIELD MAP.

This Last Supper is celebrated on battle-fields and in military cemeteries.

At the outset, of course, as usual, I know nothing. Then something begins to take shape, and suddenly an idea comes very quickly. . .

The family at the table, as usual. As if glued to it.
Snatches of the usual wretched bickering, reproaches, rebukes, anxieties. . .
The soldiers in the corner; they strike the same attitudes as in the first scene, but a little more relaxed, they are installed in the corner and nobody is going to shift them.
In the middle of the room the body of the Priest lies on the floor, arrayed for the coffin. . . .
The family squabble shamelessly over the will.
The Little Rabbi bursts in. He is in despair. He sings his lugubrious threnody,
the vulgar song from a dubious cabaret.
The soldiers take aim.
A volley of shots.
The Rabbi falls to the ground.
The dead Priest then slowly rises to his feet. Evidently he heard, in the next world, the shots fired at the Rabbi, and has come back to help him in his hour of need; he has difficulty lifting him, doing it with great care. The Rabbi comes to, and the Priest, reassured, goes back to resting in peace. The Rabbi, delighted, starts up his miserable cabaret song all over again.
The soldiers take aim.
A volley of shots.
The Rabbi falls to the ground.
The dead Priest, indefatigable, rises and lifts the body of the Rabbi.

A third time this happens, and the Priest has yet again performed his act of succour for his little friend.
The little Rabbi abruptly capitulates.
At the same moment

the soldiers begin to move,
a caterpillar-like movement
a sort of palpitation
or spasm,
as if an electric charge had passed through them.
Their faces become animated,
their mouths open,
their eyes swivel round, then their hands and feet,
repulsively,
like overwound clockwork,
they totter,
lift their legs stiffly,
place one gingerly before the other,
as if trying to remember how,
tormenting themselves,
horribly self-important.
The impression is disagreeably overblown,
tragic,
as of children or paralytics
or the dead.

The family in disgust shuts them from view with the wardrobe. But they scramble out from behind this wardrobe. The family decides to move.
It is like an evacuation.
The Uncles tug at the Aunts;
they hastily shift
the table and the chairs.
Uncle Olek stays behind, weighed down with chairs,
shouting *Karol, Józka,*
they urge each other on,
scurrying in disarray into the antechamber,
behind the door,
where *at once*
they start up all over again their cantankerous and vociferous discussion. Meanwhile the Mańka-Rabbi character has undergone another metamorphosis behind the wardrobe.
Now, strutting like a wooden doll, s/he emerges as
Mańka-Himmler.
Still strutting, s/he marches
and leads out the wretched soliders
from behind the wardrobe.
S/he marches at their head.
The march routine is carried out with a lot of (obvious) difficulty,
With many tumbles, knocks, and collisions.

But the family have had enough of life behind the door.
They slowly squeeze back into the room.

And in the general commotion:
THE SOLDIERS laboriously drag along their carcasses, legs, and feet — a tragi-comic agony which
reminds them of their 'real' life
THE TENANTS OF THE ROOM, THE FAMILY, even in the upheaval and chaos of what seems to be a
wartime evacuation still remembering their shameful little habits,
there forms, towards the rear of the stage, and gradually,
a semicircle
including everyone.
They are all mixed up together,
absurdly
made equal,
as at the Last Judgement,
the pimping uncles,
prostitutes,
the possessed,
clowns,
deserters,
absentees,
recruits,
the condemned men, naked wretches,
the Priest and his double
Nurse with the Corpse (formerly the photographer's widow)
and then
there emerges
yet another spectral figure —
the fiddler-deportee — the invalid with the crutch.
He makes elaborate preparations to perform for such a large audience.
But the old violin case is empty.
His fraudulent gestures do no good
all he can play is the fool – the miserable old convict.
At last he has to take hold of his shamefully exposed
crank
and turn it.
The carol
from Chopin's B Minor Scherzo
mangled
by his hurdy-gurdy.
Everyone waits and waits. . .
Maybe it will never happen, this
Last Supper
but instead

Christmas Eve
with carols.
They all begin moving forward
very slowly.
The Uncles unroll an army map
like a long tablecloth,
and already they are all crowding round
the field table.
The Priest, in the middle, opens his arms in the familiar gesture.
There is no longer room for doubt
that this is to be
The Last Supper,
Ultima Cena.
Laymen enact apostolic gestures,
soldiers
caught in some final
fatal thrust
fall one after the other —
and
then
the tablecloth falls — the army map,
they all freeze, gesturing
in the void,
the soldiers are lifeless
shrivelled —
Nurse with the Corpse gives a ghastly smile.

The Scene of The Last Supper

May 8, 1980

Before the rehearsal, I read my actors the plan I have devised for the score of 'The Last Supper'. Then we began to rehearse, and to build up the dramatic situation.
Everything in the written text that was startling and disturbing failed to achieve the desired effect of suspense in the actors' run-through. The intensity was not there. To evoke it I would have had to employ a quite different technique and a different style of acting, one both narrative and illustrative. And this was the source of my confusion. Narrative techniques, or story-telling, and illustrative techniques *a fortiori*, are alien to Cricot's methods.
I make quite radical changes to the plan in the course of the rehearsal itself. And I am convinced yet again that the nature of my work rules out the possibility of writing a 'score' before rehearsing. The rehearsal itself, with its spontaneous and abrupt decisions, thoughts, and actions, constitutes the

'writing' of the score. After which it needs only to be transcribed. To shatter this ubiquitous image of 'The Last Supper' I decide to elevate it even higher, towards the regions of even greater purity of form. For that reason the table must be covered with a spotlessly white starched tablecloth, with the traces of folds clearly visible.

Such a table emerges downstage, covered with the white cloth.

And now I compose the picture without any actors.

Just four naked dummies, right at the back, pressed tightly together.

It is my experience that to position them in a row lends them rhythmic and expressive power.

Scattered about the stage, they were naturalistic. The same is true of the crosses. There are a dozen or so of these.

They are churchyard crosses. I place them in front of the dummies as on military graves in a cemetery. Then the DUMMIES of the Priest and Helka, seated on chairs. Then the live Helka.

Next comes a row of chairs for the FAMILY.

And lastly the TABLE.

That is the way it ought to look, finally.

Initially, none of this exists.

It will fall to the FAMILY to solemnly set the scene, concentrating hard, with some *mysterious* DESIGN, whose point we do not know, acting with great precision as if something crucial depended upon their performance. This goes on for a longish time, it constitutes an obscure *preparation* for something, something MUST HAPPEN, something is IMMINENT, they even introduce the soldiers, carrying them on like graveyard monuments, adjusting the position of arms and legs . . .

It would seem now that everything is finished,

and that this order of things will last for all time.

Now everything is almost ready.

The FAMILY sits down at the TABLE, on stools.

Their gestures grow more and more obviously like those in 'The Last Supper'.

But they are still not perfect copies.

The family of course goes on with its violent and scandalous quarrel over the will, a sort of ancient threnody, recriminations, reproaches. The Father-on-Leave swears like a trooper,

Helka, beside herself, repeats over and over again some phrases from her unhappy marriage rite.

The Little Rabbi (Judas at the same time) wails something indistinctly, perhaps his *Rebecca* chant.

Suddenly Uncle Stasio comes in, the exile,

beggar and tinker, the black sheep of the family.

They all recognize him.

Despite the fact that he has already been before in different surroundings and scenes, in the present order of things, where TIME seems to the spectators like ETERNITY — this recollected frame appearing at the very end is the

FIRST FRAME.

Uncle Stasio starts playing: it is his last concert.

CAROL.

Is this 'Last Supper' actually Christmas?

This melody evidently possesses some kind of fatal power for suddenly, at the back of the stage, the soldiers begin stirring ominously, coming to life.

This ORDER established with such care begins to abruptly fall apart, to break down,

a frightening turmoil of naked bodies, SOLDIERS, rifles, CROSSES.
Everything collapses at the back of the stage, one huge cemetery.
Downstage the 'Last Supper' runs its course.
The CAROL continues.
The FAMILY, calmly at first, clears the TABLE,
arranges the chairs, and withdraws.
But their departure gradually turns into flight, evacuation, catastrophe, the end of the world.
They push, fall, crawl, drag corpses, wounded, crosses, all their goods and chattels. . .
The PRIEST remains on the empty stage — the POLISH SORROWING CHRIST.

The Scene of The Last Supper

May 8, 1980

I am still not happy with the way this scene has gone in rehearsal up to now.
Immediately before the next rehearsal I shall draw up a new plan. Leonardo's painting, which I
have always deeply admired, arouses in me a sort of perverse urge to desecrate its superhuman
order and calm, and to bring it down to earth by means of an act of violence.

The FAMILY squabble shamelessly over the will
a scene which becomes hellish, nightmarish.
A CIRCUS cum BROTHEL.
THE BED cum DEATH-MACHINE runs through its paces.
They turn it faster and faster.
Now the DUMMY Priest appears,
now the LIVE ACTOR.
The Family splits into two camps.
One accepts the authenticity of the Dummy,
the other, the Live Actor.
They keep turning, faster and faster.
The quarrel becomes more and more violent.

They throw the Live Priest to the floor,
Stretch him out.
Simulated lamentation.
They stand over the grave.
Carefully erect a cross.
The ceremony of the BURIAL.

The LITTLE RABBI's outrageous intervention.
The RABBI's despair.

The MUSIC-HALL song about REBECCA.
Entry of the FIRING SQUAD.
The LITTLE RABBI falls.
THE PRIEST rises from the dead to help the LITTLE RABBI.
THE RABBI departs for good.
Suddenly everything begins to *decay* on the stage.
In this ROOM,
there is a kind of general malfunctioning of the works.
The SOLDIERS start crawling like maggots,
aping tragicomic despair.
The FAMILY in disgust shuts out
these ALIEN TENANTS of the room by means of the WARDROBE
(the WARDROBE is a significant object in the CHILDHOOD ROOM).

Mad Auntie Mańka has undergone a new transformation,
she appears as a monstrous NAZI DOLL
Looking like HIMMLER, she struts like a child in fancy dress.
She heads the ARMY
of lead soldiers,
dead,
screaming,
in their death throes,
mixed up with NAKED CONDEMNED MEN,
with CROSSES torn from graves,
a troupe of CRIPPLES
KILLED IN ACTION.

PANIC.
A stampede of EVACUEES,
FLIGHT,
DISASTER,
the cries of the FAMILY,
a total *breakdown*,
disintegration,
exposure,
now we can see who these dignified NEAREST AND DEAREST really are,
wage-slaves loaned out
by the STAGE ACTORS' HIRE DEPARTMENT
not relatives at all,
they are not even acquainted.
The Uncles are dirty pimps.
Helka is a whore,
Józka an escapee from a home for perverts,
Mańka from a lunatic asylum.

The Father-on-Leave is a deserter,
Grandma a skivvy
and the recruits
naked corpses.
Each one tries to be something different,
each advertises his wares as if in the market-place,
a monstrous CIRCUS,
A FLEA MARKET of lousy actors
posturing like marionettes,
A HELL, A WHOREHOUSE,
THE LAST JUDGEMENT,
THE APOCALYPSE,
utter licentiousness.
On the bed Auntie Józka and the exile, now naked.
Helka stands astraddle the thing labelled Golgotha.
Auntie Mańka reaches religious orgasm with the DUMMY Priest.
The DUMMY Helka is raped by the SOLDIERS,
actors climaxing on chairs,
orgasmic movements,
plenty of CROSSES,
as in a graveyard.

Into all this the PRIEST walks slowly.
At the same time the EXILE's weird accoutrement appears,
the VIOLIN CASE plays its CAROL.

Slowly in the general LEVELLING DOWN of this hellish circus
a REPRODUCTION appears, a dim reflection
of the familiar picture of The Last Supper.
The soldiers perform rifle-drill over the long table.
The 'civilians' (the FAMILY) vainly imitate the gestures of the apostles.

In this way this (hopefully) LAST supper is celebrated,
while the CAROL makes it seem like Christmas Eve. . .

The Scene of The Last Supper

Friday, May 30, 1980

I had more or less made up my mind, that the last version of 'The Last Supper' was the definitive one. Yet I still want to give free play to my imagination. I certainly have no intention of mounting a rehearsal of 'The Last Supper'. I simply want to check the functioning of the table and its collapsible metal legs. The table should not really *be* a table at first. It must be brought onstage in the form of two very long and dirty unplaned planks, of the kind the bricklayers use as scaffolding. The soldiers bring in the planks. It looks as if they might be used to screen a building site. They put them down. Only after all this do the FAMILY suddenly pick them up, quickly open out the metal legs hidden under them, and lay the table they have made with an immaculately white tablecloth.

But now I don't like these metal supports. I have them removed. We are left with two bare planks. I wonder what to do with them. Someone takes them off. Their time will come. But this does not set my mind at rest. I am very anxious to find another solution to the problem of the TABLE. This *object* is crucial to 'The Last Supper'. I move the chairs, as in the last version, to the front of the stage, and behind them I arrange the naked mannequins, like naked convicts, with a cemetery full of crosses behind them, and the SOLDIERS last of all.

Just their rifles, with fixed bayonets, stick out.

But now I have to work out all the other positions.

The FAMILY, in its entirety, seats itself downstage in the chairs.

The whole stage seems to be WAITING for something.

Suddenly the two UNCLES run off.

They re-appear a moment later, staggering under the weight of an enormously long PLANK.

They have to force their way through the serried ranks of people, chairs, and naked soldiers. They are oblivious to everything. They elbow aside or overturn everything in their path. The Priest falls to the ground. Naked mannequins, stools, and people roll around in confusion.

Right behind them, two soldiers appear with another, similar PLANK. The two planks sway dangerously on the heads of the actors.

It looks as if these two heavy, dirty, and mud-stained objects, brought from God knows-where or for what purpose, will fall on to the stage any minute, squashing and smashing everyone and everything.

The planks eventually land downstage, they come to rest on something or other, or perhaps the actors themselves even keep hold of them.

General chaos. Everything totters and sways.

Massed choirs intoning a PSALM lend an ecclesiastical air to the proceedings. Amid the growing disorder the FAMILY keeps up its long-standing quarrel, its lamentations and recollections, but accelerated, somehow, as if SOMETHING threatened to cut them short. Extravagant gestures accompany their repulsive squabbling, but they are so deliberate that they seem already to foreshadow The Last Supper.

Naked soldiers throng shamelessly round them.

The Army downstage is evidently getting out of hand, their malfunctioning clockwork is beginning to run out of control, destructively.

They push the WARDROBE to the very front of the stage, showing no consideration for the actors, thrusting it over the footlights, right under the noses of the audience.

A WINDOW, TABLE, CHAIRS and BED are pushed on from the other side; the soldiers turn the crank of the violin case.

The exile-cum-pedlar, taking advantage of the confusion, elbows his way through to the front, behind the window, and gets ready for his gimcrack concert.

The PHOTOGRAPHER wheels in her CAMERA, then the PRAM WITH THE CORPSE.

The WARDROBE opens right in front of the audience, not just from the front but from the back as well, and soldiers rush through it.

The pace is hotting up, as in some diabolical cabaret, shameless, naked mannequins are dragged around and wallow on the floor, the PRIEST and his DUMMY/DOUBLE lie on the floor, trampled on.

The PSALM gives way to a MARCH.

THOSE around the table assume the unmistakable postures of da Vinci's 'Last Supper'.

The EXILE-cum-BUSKER begins his last concert.

THE CAROL.

The actors slowly leave the stage, moving towards the back, looking round, gradually disappearing, one after the other.

The PRIEST remains.

I take him by the hand and we slowly walk off together.

Then I come back, fold up the tablecloth with infinite care,

put it under my arm

and exit.

The Artist and the Theatre

The Condition of the Artist

The 'condition' of the artist is uncommon. To clarify this doubtless banal proposition I shall have to compose a whole lot more fine phrases and sentences.

Of course I do not set the artist on a pedestal. The condition of any individual, from the simplest to the most complex, may, like that of the artist, have 'no exit' inscribed on it.

But the condition of the artist is special, because if we try to *compare* him with other people, we will find ourselves reaching down into the dark and secret places.

The condition of the artist is *circumscribed*. His confinement is fundamental to his existence, it exerts a powerful fascination while at the same time cutting him off from every kind of unambiguous, simple, superficial approach to the world. It may well be that this limitation, this *constriction*, is a major criterion of truth.

As a child, I used to make cakes out of paper. These cakes were two-dimensional. But I was oblivious to the fact. I used to cut them in slices. It took me a terribly long time to realize that there was something missing, the absence of which made slicing impossible. So then I stopped making paper cakes and fell from that state of grace and favour which can only be compared to 'the condition of the artist'.

This *absence* or *lack* is precisely the confinement of which I spoke.

A confinement in the eyes of the world, naturally.

The artist has to pay for this strange privilege of operating 'beyond' life. The condition of the artist is like that of someone, who,

striving towards some particularly significant goal,
suddenly senses that the act of pressing onward
is the essence of his quest and the point of his existence.
And — looking for a way out, or just a way through,
realizes
that around him more and more doors are shutting,
that he must shut many of them himself,
try another way,
press on,
in the full and terrifying knowledge that everything is a Void,
that the real nature of his task
is to close doors, thereby
shutting off
shutting out everything
that ceaselessly tries to furnish the Void with a content,
that passes under the name of Reality,
arrogating to itself the only valid universality
and all legitimacy pertaining thereto . . .
And only when the holocaust happens,
When our vaunted 'reality' dissolves,
amid disgrace and denunciation, clutching at words

to describe itself: 'it all turned out to be a fabrication',
amid the babble of mutual contradictions and alternative strategies —
the 'condition of the artist' draws close to the moment
of self-revelation. But it is already too late.
And in any case, nobody has been listening.

The Work of Art and the Creative Process

The act of writing a book, composing a symphony, or painting a picture is acknowledged to be a creative process, and thus a unique and privileged manifestation of the human spirit. For this reason, it may seem strange that the *perception* of this uncommon process occurs only after it has been *extinguished*. For what is actually *consumed* is merely its *product*, in the form of a book, the orchestral performance of a work, an exhibited picture.

The actual creative process remains inaccessible to us. To state this at its most extreme, we may say that in the reception of the work of art there is a paradoxical cancelling out of the most inspired, the most spiritual, moment: of the whole mystery of creativity.

Only the trace left by this process is fed to the consumer, he gnaws on its imprint like a dog chewing a bone, desperate to find in it some image of the Great Explosion. Quite fruitlessly.

When I first discovered this way of looking at things, I was dazzled by the freshness and unambiguousness of it. The result was my *Popular Exhibition*, 1963. THE WORK, or material product of the creative process, seemed to me questionable and institutionalized.

I made up my mind to place in the foreground that creative moment which had hitherto been discreetly erased from memory, blocked from the gaze of the spectators, so as not to detract from the greatness of the work itself — conceived of as a monument.

I recognized as creativity everything that partook of that turbulent and inchoate moment.

It might all be, as regards the details, unpolished, lacking in refinement, poorly integrated, even something to be ashamed of, without rhyme or reason, all over the place — yet original despite everything, quite unlike anything else, the irreducible stuff of *creativity*.

Bric-a-brac, all of it, generally consigned to the deepest recesses of a forgotten drawer, never to see the light of day.

This was my own invention, this recognition of the artistic status of great tracts of the 'attics' of consciousness, the *ingredients* of memory, this consecration of what might be called the *lumber-room* of our conscious activities. A very personal aspect was given to all this by virtue of the fact that the occasion of these obscure and to a certain extent forbidden practices was my 'official' artistic output.

The production of these works of art (painting pictures) was a sort of atavistic act, a kind of magic ritual. If I had dropped it I would have risked losing my powers altogether.

Carrying on was a way of ensuring that life went on.

These 'official' or 'ritualistic' works were the pretext for the initiatives I have referred to, those of a 'lower order', which were promoted, by a conscious decision on my part, to the status of serious art.

I use the word 'personal' because what I am talking about is a weak and vulnerable part of myself, one moreover which I do not wish to repudiate.

I continue to produce those 'official' works. Perhaps I do it for my own personal pleasure, or to satisfy some need, or perhaps I do it because I am looking for a pretext. Perhaps I don't even take them very seriously, they are (if you like) just cardboard shams and replicas to entice and ensnare.

I throw up this smokescreen of seriousness around my works so as to catch (as in a mousetrap) all the incandescent particles of imagination, of scepticism, of resolution, of capitulation, of rapture, of euphoria, which are generated by the actual process of creation. This 'illicit' manipulation of my own 'official' reality, my realistic 'front', continues to fascinate me by virtue of its potential for mystification and perversity.

I am devoting so much time to these matters because I am anxious to differentiate between my own case and a widespread trend which you can look up in any encyclopedia of contemporary art under the heading *Process Art*.

As I was saying:

The fruits of my experience, contained in the *Anti-exhibition*, is a way of taking issue with the WORK OF ART (e.g. the picture) as the *terminus ad quem* of certain artistic procedures. My taste for mystification turns the work of art into an atavistic ritual (maybe a sort of 'domestic altar') and mousetrap — sham, sprung to catch those elusive devices and techniques, that chaotic turmoil of ideas, imagination, consciousness, all wildly mixed up with the raw materials of life, the whole scandalous *bricolage* dignified by the name of the creative process.

Secondly: the conclusions of the *Anti-exhibition* had nothing in common with the doctrinaire programme of a trend which, supplanting THE WORK, proclaimed the effective sublimation of formal elements by means of a completely AUTONOMOUS STRUCTURE, the essence of which is simply PROCESS. My conception was very much more complex. It consisted in a totality of innumerable actions of different sorts, performed with impetuosity and passion, but by no means 'self-sufficient', because some distant OBJECTIVE could be sensed in them, the possibility of some great CONSUMMATION, the PRESENTIMENT of an outline of some QUINTESSENTIAL FORM, some CULMINATION, TERMINATION, or WORK. It was part of my intention to reject the idea of the END and the CLOSED WORK OF ART, so as to deny myself the satisfaction of a SOLUTION. Nothing should remain but REHEARSALS, and only REHEARSALS: Just normal rehearsals, often unsuccessful, full of mistakes, corrections, changes, alternative versions, and snags. We must acknowledge the REHEARSAL, with its intensity and agitation, as true art.

To strip the REHEARSAL of its objective and its point may be *unimaginable*, *absurd*, *heretical*, or even *nihilistic*.

Yet it must be stripped of its objective!

This is the price we must pay for the discovery of a NEW STRUCTURE, within the confines of which the spectator's imagination will itself compose both the FORM and the CONTENT of something which will no longer be called a WORK OF ART.

A brief digression on the subject of the art of the actor, which some fools think of simply as a kind of imitation, or which they deny any right to be called art at all. Actually disputes of this kind are prehistoric and lack any sort of contemporary relevance. They start from the premise that the actor only interprets a part already composed by the author. But relying only on common sense criteria, we could equally say that a painter merely imitates when he paints somebody's portrait: since, of course, it was not the painter who made the actual person, but the parents who begot him. If we approach the problem from a more theoretical standpoint, we should bear in mind that the popular opinion that the author is the *raison d'être* of the theatre has already been challenged on a number of occasions.

I do not intend to derive any system of rules from these observations. That would be naive. But it does seem to me that belief in the indispensible presence of the author has ceased to be a real issue in the theatre.

The author of the text is by no means the one who runs the show.

The idea of a self-referential theatre is always worth keeping in mind, especially in a period of critical impotence and decadence. There is no sensible reason for handing over that particular trump card.

These deliberations are not the outcome of some urge to belittle the author. Far from it. I have always been an advocate of the text as an indispensable condensation of reality. Indeed, I was probably the only one who, at the time when happenings were all the rage, discovered that an artistically composed reality (as, for instance, in Rembrandt's *Anatomy Lesson*) may be treated as a 'readymade' (*'l'objet prêt'*) — and I made use of it with particular satisfaction. The author's text has, in my view, a 'reality' of this kind.

In *Cricot 2* productions, the literary text is distinct from the visual presentation and treated as one semantic element, in a manner consistent with its structure and function. But it is not fundamental to the action of the show or the actors' performances. Indeed, these are altogether independent and built up in accordance with the creative potential of the actor.

The Miracle of the Real

The miraculous side of the theatre and the stage (and for that matter of art as a whole) comes from what is material and real. Such has been my assumption from the outset — an absolute, perfectly unborrowed article of faith. If I were to paint a certain landscape, I would do so without getting carried away by nature; rather I would take extra pains to macerate the canvas before me, so that it would itself turn into a landscape.

I have always rejected the will-o'-the-wisp side of the theatre, the common phantasmagoria of dazzling light effects, or gauze curtains, or magic shifts of decor which pretend to be something else than they actually are, trapdoors and other notorious exits into a secure space, where ILLUSION suffers a vile humiliation.

And yet, rejecting illusion, I do treat it as a serious adversary. It is the pundits of the Theatre, especially, who connive at the disgraceful practice of procuring Illusion. Illusion should emerge from the Real! It is perfectly all right for Illusion to arise from the manipulation of the Real. But then Illusion becomes something else, a metaphor, an atmosphere, a symbol. . .

As to the actor's illusionism, his struggle to present emotional states — depressions, obsessions, hallucinations — in the 'appropriate' mode (known as ACTING) — all this is to me but a gross and sickening form of SIMULATION. I propose a different approach in which the actual HANDLING of the REAL, of true OBJECTS, is allowed.

This means the REIFICATION of the mental sphere, of the emotions, the inner life, and so a purification of acting from its unbearable psychologism and titillation. This means, furthermore, the facilitation of arbitrary situations — things incomprehensible, shocking, impossible, often with an air of the circus or a symbol about them. And it means the creation of objects — bizarre, mysterious, enigmatic — yet objects all the same.

Last of all, this method expects an actor to go back on the essence of acting, if acting is understood as the expression, or, to put it bluntly, imitation of the psychological states of the represented characters. But to confine the name of ACTING to such a posture is improper. ACTING can be something very different. It can be a distinctive form of behaviour closely related to a real activity, discarding psychological underpinnings.

The Theatre of Place

**Removing the dividing line
between the stage and the auditorium**

The idea of the material penetration of art into life has led to the removal of hitherto existing barriers between them.

Art has ceased to be the reflection of life, or the illusion of life.

It has become, in relation to life, a kind of trial run, or a hypothesis, a manifesto or an analogical structure. It no longer demands contemplation, but cognition. The great barrier in the theatre was the footlights and the curtain. These have been removed. The outcry which greeted their removal brought to mind the storming of the Bastille. Theatrical ILLUSIONISM has indeed been overthrown. Perhaps the faith in its magical efficacy had already waned with the *ancien régime*. The bare POSTERIORS of the set were hastily exposed, together with all the apparatus thereunto. The walls of Elsinore collapsed on the spot. In their place appeared 'working' constructions, erected with enthusiasm, platforms, ladders, staircases, drivebelts — all serving to coordinate movement and action.

A less radical initiative was the replacement of illusion by allusion, minimal information, or a self-referential image inspired by Cubism. — In the current jargon, theatre historians call these transformations *removing the dividing line between the stage and the auditorium*. The removal was aided and abetted by a revolutionary era which proclaimed and foresaw active participation on the part of a public which up to then had remained passive, as well as (the other side of the coin) the possibility, indeed necessity of the actor making direct contact with the spectator. The distance separating the stage from the auditorium had to be removed — and removed it was. Illusion, which contributed to the sense of distance and was conditioned by the very existence of that dividing line, had to be abolished. Their place was taken by apparatus, which came to be known as 'the fittings', a structure implementing the intentions of the play, the dramatic action, and the performances of the actors.

When the Curtain neither Rises nor Falls, or, Much Ado About Illusion and Fiction

Under the naturalistic dispensation full-blown *illusion* coexisted with full-blown *fiction*. Once the theatre-goer's mind had been set at rest, and he was quite sure that the events unfolding within the framework of the box stage were fiction and only fiction, he could relax and enjoy *watching*. Nothing more was required of him!

But this kind of passive receptivity to naturalistic illusion eventually came to seem inadequate, even trivial.

A need was felt, and felt more and more acutely, for greater involvement of the spectator in the spectacle. This also happened in other artistic spheres.

It became apparent that the work of art could not remain what it had been; its function and structure had to change.

It ceased to be a *reflection* of life, confining the aesthetic response to secure *observation*, leaving the spectator untroubled and untouched.

Increasingly, dramatic productions would come as a challenge, a provocation, an accusation, demanding from the spectator an immediate response, pressing him for a judgement. They would be addressed straight at him, the spectator. And he would no longer be able to avoid taking some stand towards the events on the stage.

Illusion, which kept all this at a safe distance, had to go. The buffer zone, in the form of footlights, proscenium, and pit, everything which (like the moat at the zoo) ensured the safety of the audience, was removed.

Freed from its illusory backdrops, the dramatic action advanced to meet the audience.

Trompe l'oeil landscapes and phantom buildings became superfluous. Bare boards, a platform or two, some steps, were just as good.

The acting too, hitherto contained within the 'fourth wall', turned to meet the spectator, even became a sort of assault on his susceptibilities.

So from one standpoint, the real target of this theatrical *coup d'état* was the spectator, who was now expected to *relate* actively to what was happening on the stage, to the show. Or, to put it bluntly, to the *fiction*!

Ideally, this ought to have turned the spectator into a participant. In what, exactly? In the fiction, in the deception!

On the other hand, the fictional world had to be brought closer to the real world, so as to produce the illusion that we were dealing with real life (sic!).

In the first instance, the problem was to obliterate the division between the stage and the audience, to eliminate all the paraphernalia of illusion.

The action and the audience would no longer occupy separate spaces; parts of the stage were located among the audience, or the spectators seated in the midst of the acting space. If it was a hospital, the audience would be seated right next to patients' beds; if a prison, then you might be sharing a cell with the inmates; you would be so close to a rioting mob on the streets that you would feel the urge to join in. . . .

(Of course you never would).

Or, in a different kind of environment, the spectator might be placed amidst authentic furniture in a drawing room, as described in the stage directions. Yet for all its real furniture, the drawing room would not be a real drawing room, it is still the *representation* of a drawing room, embedded in the text of the play, in the world of fiction, in other words.

The spectator would still be the spectator, if not more so, and placed inside the décor like this would feel in the way, out of place, and either presumptuous or as embarrassed as a child.

These efforts at situating the spectator and the actor on the same 'plane' (both literally and metaphorically speaking) and granting the two the same (more or less equal) rights in the hope that the *fiction* of both play and performance would lose some of its messiness and grow more truthful, closer to real life — all this had an air of born-again-fundamentalism; like the constructivism which flourished during the Russian Revolution, with its faith in a brave new world wholly integrated with the world of art.

But when all this was simply done all over again, in our own day, by our bogus avant-garde, without understanding, or courage, or any kind of artistic scruples — it was sheer idiocy!

In the second instance, when it came to settling the account with fiction, the news is even worse. Much was done to counteract the potency of fiction. It was brought closer to life and to lived reality.

Plays would be mounted not in the theatre, but in the kind of place that the action was set in.

Toller's *Gas*, for instance, was performed in a gas chamber.

This is a trivial and naive kind of radicalism.

Despite having made a foray into real life, fiction did not cease to exist. And in any case this literal-minded tautology, this forcing of parallels between the content of a play and the real place in which it was acted, was the purest naturalism, worthy of Stanislavsky. For all the innovations, the FICTIONAL element of the play was treated as conventionally as before; its *representational* element was still very much in evidence.

And as soon as the play got going, the place would be forgotten.

Maybe you *could* say that the spectator really *had* been located at the heart of the action. But you would have to add that, in the process, the power of illusion had increased many times over. For the spectator had simply been transported to the midst of complete illusion, complete fiction. This would at once become apparent upon leaving the theatre, or rather the gas chamber: because then the illusion would fade.

When innovations like these, new methods, confrontations, were first current — during the revolutionary upheavals of the avant-garde period — there were indisputably good reasons for them, and they had the force of a genuine radicalism.

Small wonder that they excited my imagination when I was young, and I imitated them. But between 1942 and 1944 — during the war, in other words — I came to see their shortcomings and their contradictions only too clearly.

A Critique of Constructivism, or Settling my Accounts with Illusion and Fiction

At this point, having traversed the highways and byways of this lengthy digression, I come back with some relief to this, the final stage of my odyssey, and to the beginnings of my own work in the theatre and my own conception of theatre.

In all these struggles between constructivism and illusion and fiction, every attempt to resolve the matter centred ultimately on formal issues. This is because the diametrically opposed notion, that of THE REAL, was left indistinct and ill-defined.

But THE REAL EXISTS, IN LIFE ITSELF, IN DAY-TO-DAY REALITY. The reason why all those attempts at doing away with ILLUSION and FICTION (in both the play and its presentation) failed was that they were never brought into contact with authentic REALITY.

FICTION simply had no contact with REALITY, failed to encounter its own extension there.

There was nothing REAL in all this. This 'space' was just another enclosure, cut off like some nature reserve from everyday reality, for the sake of an aesthetic experience called THEATRE.

The spectator still found himself in a space which had been annexed by theatre, an institution which specializes in the illicit traffic in fiction and the manipulation of fiction.

He was simply *deluded* into believing that, while still in the sphere of fiction, he was experiencing it as reality.

My Scorn for the Sacred Cow of Representationalism

I believe I was born with an aversion for

'representation'

FORGERY

ROLE-PLAYING

SIMULATION

of characters, heroes, situations, narratives, places, or actions.

Pretty well everything, in fact, that was considered to be the essence of the theatre and of acting, the *sine qua non* of drama,

beyond dispute —

it all smacked of counterfeit and chicanery to me.

Professionals, it goes without saying, considered this aversion of mine as bad manners, nothing more or less. That is, if they paid any attention at all: many found it very hard to credit.

My aversion had serious consequences for me: it became the formative element in my attitude to theatre, and my conception of theatre, and this was what came between me and the activities of the avant-garde of the 'twenties, with their feverish search for new methods of *presentation* and of *acting*.

My theatre was founded upon a rejection of the concept and the practice of REPRESENTATION and this meant going BEYOND the confines of theatre,
indeed a challenge to the existing theatre and its structures.

But I must add that such ideas were arrived at only very, very much later, and with unfortunate results.

LET ME REMIND YOU OF THE DATE: 1944!

I may say that my transgressions against the universal code of theatrical practices — which it would be impossible to chronicle in full — not only place me beyond the pale of contemporary professional theatre, but also exclude me from the ranks of those who call themselves avant-garde, where *illusion* and *fiction* are gathering momentum in a veritable avalanche of representationalism.

A Minor Digression

In this anti-theatrical activity of mine, which you can call — if you want to —
dissent,
heresy,
protest,
I was simply trying to discover another route to the theatre.

I needed to find a completely different way of articulating and implementing a passion which, despite everything, I solemnly believe was intrinsically theatrical.

Dramatic Fiction must Enter our Lives

My attitude to the world of the play — to its domains of imagination, to its fictionality — to its secret, magical powers — was characterized, one might say, by an ardent, even if naive, faith.

I firmly believed that what was happening in the play was happening 'for real', all around me, in everyday life.

And it was *theatre* I blamed for producing such a poor imitation, such a deceitful copy, of that authentic realm.

I felt that there was something degrading and unworthy about diminishing the nobility and the truth of the play by means of all those cheap tricks, cramping the style of the heroes, giving them gestures and words *which were not their own*, forcing them to *play a part*. . .

In my feverish *état d'âme* of those days, I gradually ceased to distinguish between fiction and life in the creative process. It all took place on the boundaries of imagination and life.

I started believing that characters from the play were going to reappear as part of my life — or of *our* life — that they would come back and dwell among us for a certain time; something was calling to me from the past, invoking the rites of the dead, the ceremony of All Souls, Poland's *zaduszki* . . . . Perhaps all I had to do was to use a little magic. . .

I seemed to see my *dramatis personae* all around me, disappearing round a street corner, in a dimly lit cafe, in the stairwell of some block of flats, in the corner of a courtyard. . . They were busy doing something, but I was sure that they knew they were being watched, and that I was following them. . . They were in no way different in appearance from other passers-by, from us.

It was obvious to me that these *revenants* from the world of the play could not be thought of as SHADES (even though, as it turned out much later in *Dead Class*, they had a lot in common with the dead): they had to be LIVING people. LIVING not only in the biological sense, but in a 'social' sense too.

Belonging, that is, to our life and time,

part and parcel of our everyday life,

our all-too-human condition,

and a part of our PLACE, of the space we occupy in our everyday lives.

PLACE!

That was the word I needed, the one I thought might offer a solution to this otherwise impossible dilemma.

I had to reckon with the fact that despite my 'metaphysical' view of drama its basic content is FICTION.

The point was, however, to turn the dramatic fiction into its opposite. To bring it into clandestine contact with the realities of life, with our everyday life.

This would ensure its *continuity*, its continued existence in the world of the living. Which recalls an ancient belief that a demon can enter the body of a living being, and speak and act through him.

Challenging Artistic Space
Theatrical Spaces amid the Realities of Life

This was a major step forward in the formation of my conception of theatre. Again I recall the date, the year: 1944!

This discovery shook the entire illusion of the holy altar of art to its foundations, with its aroma of incense and all its sacred mysteries. It was not a simple matter, mind you, to utter that seemingly simple proposition: 'the theatre is the least appropriate place for the presentation of drama.'

The theatre, a place sealed off from the bustle of everyday life, a sanctuary, something like a museum, set aside for the presentation and reception of FICTION, proved an unsuitable place for the desired *encounter* of fiction and life. It was quite clear that this act of copulation between fiction and life, so to speak, could be located only META-THEATRICALLY, in the midst of life itself. And it was equally clear that what was needed was something different from the well-known practice of transferring a dramatic narrative from the theatre building to some 'authentic' site:

The forecourt of the cathedral, where a mystery play might merge into a church service, or

castle battlements, to make ghosts look more plausible, or

in the market square, to enliven some public festivity.

All this adds up to no more than choosing a picturesque, strange, or mysterious setting, which, apart from introducing a touch of 'atmosphere', is altogether irrelevant to the action of the play.

Tricks like these can never be more than displays of pretentious and misguided 'artistry'.

And if I dwell upon them at such length, it is only because they represent a facile sort of *stylization* which is easily confused by popular opinion with genuine innovation, and too often passes for the real thing.

The Scandalous Clash of Dramatic Fiction with Place

So if I was trying to find a location for the drama and its imaginative structures outside of the theatre, in the midst of life, it was for other, and much more fundamental, reasons than these.

By 'accepting' a place somewhere in everyday reality, dramatic fiction would ASSIMILATE ITS SHAPES, ITS PROPERTIES, ITS PERSONAGES: IT WOULD INSINUATE ITSELF INTO THE PLACE, AND VIA THIS PLACE WOULD REACH US AS TRUTH, AS REALITY. THE PLACE would serve as a FILTER.

And the Fiction would become a reality of the same order as the spectator, his world, his time.

There would be no question of constructing *parallels* or *analogies* between the place and the play. AND THIS LEADS ME TO MY NEXT DISCOVERY.

The place chosen must be incommensurate and incongruent with the substance of the play (considered as a fiction).

The narrative element of the play needs to be subjected to a semantic shift.

An effect of rupture which is startling and shocking!

This play of differences constitutes the real content, always provocative, alogical, resisting a homogenous interpretation!

Two levels of signification, each alien and hostile to the other!

And only at this juncture, as a consequence of their interpenetration, can the semantic system be actualized!

A Description of Places from 1944 to the Present Day

These are the places where my theatre was located, or that I dreamed about. I really cannot say for sure what was special about them, or what induced me to single them out.

Maybe a sort of elemental ordinariness. . .

a familiarity. . .

a forlornness. . .

nostalgia, melancholy, sadness. . .

transitoriness . . . poetry
a rooted sorrow, 'poverty' . . . .

No doubt my choice was influenced by my own proclivity from the outset for the notion which I have termed REALITY OF THE LOWEST ORDER, the basis of which is, as I emphasized in my *emballages* manifesto, that the object discloses its real identity on the threshold of annihilation, at a point between the RUBBISH DUMP and ETERNITY.

THE RAILWAY STATION   people waiting for their trains as if awaiting fate itself, those bidding farewell and those bidden, the 'spectators' waiting and the awaited 'actors' . . . During the war I waited for Odysseus to return to his homeland and step out of a railway carriage . . .

THE POST OFFICE   with stacks of postbags, bundles, parcels, packets, a thousand units of *information*, all anonymous, caught in a state of weightlessness somewhere between the sender and the addressee . . .

RUINED, BOMB-DAMAGED FLATS   the way it was every few yards during the war, walls with great holes in them and the plaster flaking off, splintered floorboards, yawning gaps, different sorts of packing-cases strewn with plaster, sand and lime (the audience sat on these), a rotten board hung from the ceiling, some sort of ship's tow-line stretched taut across this ruin, with a German loudhailer hanging from it (the kind that people called a 'barker'), in the corner a muddy wheel from a waggon, or maybe from a field-gun, the long, heavy barrel of which was supported by bricklayers' trestles like the debris of a burnt-out civilization, slicing obliquely across the room . . . This is the nightmarish place that Odysseus has returned to in 1944, not to his Ithaca.

THE POORHOUSE   VIRTUALLY A RUBBISH DUMP . . . with the remains of beds and all sorts of debris from the primitive workshops run by forced labour, half refuge, and half prison, rubble, crumbling walls . . . this was the setting for the events of Stanislaw Witkiewicz's *The Water Hen*. A party of *clochards*, tramps, eternal wanderers, and vagabonds, played the parts of the Counts, Cardinals, Bankers, stuck-up artists, homosexuals, flunkeys, English miladies, rakes and degenerates . . . .
This idea of the 'environment' (the work of art considered as *context*), an environment of wretchedness and a 'poor art', I realized fully in 1961 with my *THEATRE INFORMEL* (the play was Witkiewicz's *The Small Manor*).

THE LAUNDRY   A place where sheets etc. are washed, a sort of ritualization of the everyday, cleaning, *cleansing*, even a sort of classical catharsis, with a jumble of washtubs and bars of soap . . . piles of newspapers, soaked, laundered, dried, coarse laundresses shouting newspaper headlines, adverts, disasters, wars, funerals, weddings, births, great clouds of steam.

THE CAFE   Tables pushed together, looking rather like the tables in a mortuary, a sinister benchful of tramps, *clochards* carrying all their worldly possessions with them, in keeping with the old adage *omnia mea mecum porto*, I have named these figures (my own invention entirely) *the wayfarers and their luggage*, their luggage being made up of their vices and follies, their loves, their foibles, their obsessions — the Apache is bound for ever together with his Beloved and for ever stabs her full of knife-wounds; two Hassidim are attached inseparably to their Last Tablets of

Salvation — skilful old waiters (professionals) attend to the needs of the audience and the actors, then turn abruptly into executioners; this café-cave was the setting for scenes taken from the typical *milieu* of Witkiewicz's plays: the *salon* life of the *élite* of the *nouveau riche*, of the upper clergy, the aristocracy, and so on.

THE CLOAKROOM   A theatre cloakroom consisting of a sort of gigantic gallows of iron, with hooks and hangers, strongly resembling the kind of gear you would find in a primitive sort of butcher's shop with quarter pigs hanging from hooks. This was a fearsome piece of apparatus and the audience had to pass through it and were forced to take off their outer clothes and leave them there. Two wardrobe attendants-cum-executioners were in charge, forcing the entire action of the play to conform to their draconian laws. The whole plot of *Lovelies and Dowdies* (this was a production of Witkiewicz's play), which is set inside a palace, in a very select milieu, in an atmosphere of polite conversation, elaborate costumes, and philosophizing, unfolded therefore in a THEATRICAL CLOAKROOM, not on the STAGE, the place of divine illusion, but in its ante-chamber, the *lowest level* of the theatre.

Yet Another Definition of the Theatre

The theatre is a kind of activity situated at the furthest limits of life, where the categories and concepts of life lose their rationale and their significance,
  where
  frenzy, feverishhness, hysteria, delusion, and hallucination are life's last defences against the oncoming CIRCUS TROUPE OF DEATH,
  the BIG SHOW.
  This is *my* definition of the theatre. Poetic and mystical, yes. But theatre does not lend itself to being thought or spoken of otherwise than this.
  Which is why my work in the theatre lacks any rational or practical schema which might readily serve as the basis for five-finger exercises. To work in the theatre means
  to *create*,
  indeed it is no less than demiurgy, its roots go deep into the 'beyond'.

After all these lengthy accounts and analyses of my original conception, which I call *Theatre of Real Place*, I again feel the need to adumbrate — for the nonce — a kind of schema of my theatrical activity.
  I have come to the conclusion that however many times I explain this strange and intricate process, both to myself and to others, I can never make it clear enough.
  Anyway, every interpretation comes after the event.
  The territory annexed by the schema already lies in bondage.
  Everything there is orderly. Nothing more is required but to verify the facts yet again. Except that despite all, something is always left hanging, something with a will of its own which may turn into the beginnings of some new development.

And besides, my schema will itself be equally mystical and poetic.

The Concept of the Theatre of Real Place

Outline of Procedure

Two personal factors have shaped my conception of the theatre. One is my deep-seated conviction that *drama* is not just a literary structure, but composes, first and foremost, a fictive order, an imaginative reality.

The other is my aversion for representationalism and my determination to root it out altogether from my work in the theatre.

The Fictive World of the Play is the World of the Dead

Thus I devised two different versions of the significance of the drama. The first went like this: the fictive system is an imaginary system (imagined, that is, and transcribed) which does not exist in the real world.

This version was, if you like, rationalist in spirit.

The other version was mystical in the extreme.

I still find it fascinating: ergo,

fictiveness is an impotent concept as far as real life is concerned by virtue of the fact that it is *void*, and therefore close to the realm of death.

For this reason I felt justified in thinking of the fictional world of drama as a DEAD WORLD inhabited by THE DEAD.

Everything else followed logically from this.

My theatre of 'the beyond' was certainly weird. There was no playhouse as such. The stage was like a graveyard full of decaying sculpture and pathetic debris, with inscriptions as on tombstones but reading: 'in the castle', 'in the forest', 'in the Square', 'in the drawing-room', 'in the harbour'. . .

The dead tirelessly *repeated* their lines, their parts, the big moments of their play over and over again *ad infinitum*, for time does not exist here. Thus they acted out anew the crises of their past lives. I assure you! And this ought to clear the way for us to grasp another point, that the 'later' plays of living, flesh-and-blood authors, of Shakespeare or of Wyspiański, are like blank cheques drawn upon the TEATRUM MORTIS.

Obviously this applies only to good writers.

It may be that all the arts operate in precisely this fashion.

The Rejection of Representationalism

The other factor that shaped my idea of the theatre derived from my aversion to 'representation', accepted at one time as a natural and inevitable feature of the theatre (or at any rate of mainstream theatre).

It is generally believed that it is the function of representation to concretize and lend substance to the fictive character of drama. But in actual fact the exact opposite happens. It simply reduplicates fiction. To be more precise: it is a counterfeit or simulation (of feelings), falsification (of spatial values). From the very outset it seemed to me that all such courses of action were ludicrous, petty, shameless. There was nothing here that I could either accept or identify with.

It was this rejection of representationalism that exerted the decisive influence on the character of my theatre. Such a thing was of course unthinkable as far as the professionals were concerned. So much the better!

Life itself is the Medium

My radical opposition to representationalism entailed a challenge to the status of the art object and (inevitably) to the work of art as such and the notion of an aesthetic *space*. The rejection of all these time-honoured shibboleths meant that I was left with the notion of WORKING WITHIN THE BOUNDS OF EVERYDAY REALITY, within life itself, in the present tense and with a place given over to the sorts of things that happen in day-to-day life. Which means the ideas discovered and worked out in the visual arts in the 1960s.

Remember my date: the year 1944.

Challenging the Aesthetic Space. Real Spaces

Operating in terms of reality rather than illusion and the fictitious had the following consequences:
    an end to the institutionalized theatrical treatment of the auditorium and the stage as places cut off from everyday life, devoted only to the fictitious and the illusory; and then
    the necessity of discovering a REAL SPACE amid everyday life, one with its own well-defined functions and properties.

The Properties of Real Places

Let us remind ourselves that in the REAL it is our task to locate something *relevant* to the drama,
to the fictitious world,
to the 'world of the Dead'
which constitutes a starting point for our otherwise controversial definitions and decisions.
For these reasons we must measure up to certain criteria;
the place chosen in 'real life' must on no account be *congruent* with the fictitious place. We are not trying to find *analogies*. Quite the reverse. The further apart they are, the more completely opposed, the more the contradictions are exposed, the more inevitably will this *incongruity* give rise to
an effect of
strangeness.
So much the stronger and more striking will be the apprehension, from
one standpoint, of THE CONCRETE MATERIALITY OF PLACE,
and on the other, the experience of the BEYOND,
THE WORLD OF THE DEAD.

Choreographing Real Space

We have to find a *choreography* appropriate to a given PLACE, the actions proper to it, its atmosphere, the characteristics emanating from it, its aura . . . This is, as it were, the 'plot' proper to a PLACE, and in addition
the raw material of the show, something with a life of its own.

The Daily Grind and how the Theatre of the Dead Disrupts it.

The idea of the REAL PLACE, first advanced by me in 1944, had two sides to it, and two corresponding stages of development.
The first was my discovery that everyday reality may serve as the material for a work of art without the need for any tricks of imitation, reproduction, or interpretation.
This simple proposition represented the outcome of decisions of considerable significance and radical import:
A deconstruction of the *work of art* and of structures which were 'artistically', or synthetically, composed;

its replacement by a *real object*, 'raw', taken straight from life;
and following on from this, a deconstruction of the *aesthetic space* (the theatre or museum) and its replacement by *real spaces*, rooted in life.

It cannot be too often repeated that even when, in the sixties, ideas and theories like these became the mainspring of the development of painting, the theatre failed to grasp its opportunities, since for all the sound and fury of its declarations of intent, it remained within the parochial confines of its professional brief.

And that, in a nutshell, is why the post-war avant-garde theatre has been so superficial and ephemeral.

But to continue: the second element in this new trend was a kind of *activity*, or *functioning*, that imitated nothing, represented nothing, did not constitute any sort of play-acting, or performance, but was identical with life functions. Thus we had actions drawn from life, and just as in life they centred upon using and manipulating REAL OBJECTS and appropriating REAL SPACE. Yet because they were now isolated from their ordinary context they appeared pointless and unfulfilled, or speaking from the standpoint of life, autonomous.

And this is my first angle on REALITY and REAL SPACE, contained in my biography under the entry for the year 1944.

It was only very much later, in the sixties to be precise, that trends and initiatives of this kind became known as happenings.

So these analytical explications and retrospectives constitute an attempt on my part to reaffirm the significance of my earlier insights. The view of things given above, the first stage of my thinking, could easily have turned into doctrine or dogma, with no way forward.

But as far as I was concerned this constituted only a beginning. For it was only at this point in time that I had reached the most meaningful and enthralling stage where FICTION (the play) was superadded, almost by a mystical process to EVERYDAY REALITY, chosen in the manner that I just described. And so we come to the *Grande Entrée* of the Theatre of the Dead.

And in point of fact, this realistic DAILY GRIND was so cramped, functional, and utilitarian that the effect of disrupting it by some alien phenomenon was to construct an intervention of such strangeness and unbelievableness that it might well be taken as a sign from 'the beyond', the other world.

The Crisis of Real Space

If, after a while, I found the idea of REAL SPACE threadbare and burdensome, this may be accounted for in terms of the familiar phenomenon of the habitualizing and conventionalizing of response. This problem emerged as early as the first stage of my investigations, which I may refer to as the *happening* stage.

We should take a closer look at this.

REAL PLACES, that is, living areas delineated by utilitarian criteria (concrete, but organized and directed to a special end) — like, for example, the laundry — had a sort of monolithic quality which permeated all their parts: the environment with its objects and gadgets kept on reminding you that it was a laundry. The actors also formed part of the whole, by virtue of the fact that they performed functions and roles bound up with, and defined by, the place itself (i.e. the laundry). But the problem remained of the group of people formerly known as the audience.

Who — in this laundry — were the spectators?

Customers (i.e. of the laundry) perhaps? Sightseers? Had they come out of curiosity or simply by chance? Or were they perhaps enticed here, then caught as in a trap? Detainees! Yes! This looks like being the most effective way of thinking of them.

They were stripped of all privileges, their well-defined contractual rights as spectators, which permitted them to keep a certain distance from the events presented onstage, to pose as impartial observers or as a critical élite sitting in judgement upon the performance and the actors or even acting as arbitrators.

They were deprived of all their sacred rights (as they saw it) of being moved by 'the best that has been thought and said'. Because (again according to their own inviolable preconceptions) art exists only in order to *express* those fleeting (thank God) interludes of illusion, fiction, and the other sublimated quintessences of life.

They were seduced and abandoned with the bait of REAL SPACE, no longer fenced around with ILLUSION and DISTANCE.

They were thrust into a situation where they were forced up against the rough raw material of life, having nothing in common (if we judge by the shibboleths of aesthetics) with the work of art.

They were reduced to the level of the PLACE with all its activities — plunged unceremoniously into the materiality of life, and to make it worse, a contribution was unmistakably demanded of them.

No wonder they would become anxious or resentful — for as long as it took them to get used to the new situation. But after a while this displacement of Illusion by means of a brutal confrontation with the coarse materiality of real life became in its turn a convention, an institutionalized trick of style, and finally just a pretentious gimmick. Menacing the audience, exposing them to the unexpected, threatening their security induced a certain kind of masochistic pleasure which in the end became quite intolerable, the more so since this new kind of spectatorly satisfaction, complete with its little thrill of danger, was at bottom quite inauthentic, being generated more and more by an awareness on the part of the audience that the danger was altogether fictitious and the menace carefully contrived and counterfeit.

And that was the end of this particular venture. We had to find something new, open up fresh fields.

REALITY OF PLACE lost its credibility. It had simply turned into another fiction. This particular construction of reality had lost all point and purpose.

The Next Step: The Object

By a series of coincidences, and by the action of devouring Time, PLACE, once a sort of real matrix of THE FICTITIOUS (the play), turned instead into an oppresssively factitious, inert literalism.

The innate laws of art (inscrutable to the gaze of men) and a dose of all-too-human idiocy transformed the reality of place, by a malicious metamorphosis, into FICTION. ILLUSION, once the mirror of 'another' world and 'another' theatre, matrix of all metaphor, metamorphoses, and poetic effects, began to call for a more ephemeral and discrete *medium* — a medium which would remain in conception diametrically opposed to ILLUSION and FICTION.

Indeed, the medium as such still aligned itself with reality. Only this reality was no longer expressed by means of PLACE, imposing its own laws upon all the theatrical elements.

This newly-discovered medium was THE OBJECT, THE THING.

Self-referential and autonomous. The '*objet d'art*'.

A thing with just one distinguishing feature: living, vital organs of its own called ACTORS.

For this reason I named it the BIO-OBJECT.

BIO-OBJECTS were not just props that the actors made use of.

Nor were they bits of the decor that you could play around with.

They formed an indivisible whole with the actors.

They emanated a life of their own, self-determining, independent of the FICTION (the content) of the drama.

It was this 'life' and the ways in which it was made manifest that constituted the *real* content of the performance. Not the *plot*, but the actual *materials* of the show.

The disclosure and presentation of the 'life' of the *BIO-OBJECT was not a matter of representing* some sort of nexus of relations located beyond the object.

Its self-sufficiency was a guarantee of its *reality*!

THE BIO-OBJECT IS A WORK OF ART.

The Room. Could this be a Milestone?

THE ROOM in my show (*Wielopole/Wielopole*)
    settled down at last
    after protracted vacillation and endless changes into something in between THE REAL SPACE I have so carefully described
    and the outlined BIO-OBJECT.

The idea of the BIO-OBJECT, as a matter of fact, had become somewhat too concrete and burdensome.

The point was to construct a model of *recollection* and of *remembrance* on a far greater scale than in *Dead Class*.

Here are my reflections on this subject, culminating in the conspicuous and oft-repeated transformations of space in *Wielopole/Wielopole*.

THE ROOM cannot be a REAL SPACE (according to the scientific rules governing such things).

There is no way it can be an actual room, a certain part of the auditorium set aside for a particular purpose, for such a room could never constitute the intimate room of childhood, but would just be a public hall.

And in any case there is a more fundamental point:

The room cannot be actual — by which I mean existing in our time dimension —

for the room must be lodged in MEMORY, in RECOLLECTION,

endlessly renewed and endlessly dying,

an organic systole and diastole.

Such is the *real* structure of recollection!

Yet the ROOM, at the same time, must not be stagey

contrived within the space where the open auditorium ends and which we call the stage.

That would make it no more than a bit of scenery

destroying irrevocably

any hope of THE REAL.

Caught on the horns of this dilemma, logic capitulates unconditionally, renouncing all attempts at analytic and rational thought.

No doubt we will have to extend the boundaries of our idea of THE REAL to encompass a territory as yet not grasped materially, MEMORY.

MEMORY is acknowledged as the ONE THING REAL.

Which means we must construct a real model of MEMORY.

Its workings and its expressive resources.

In other words transpose the concept of THE REAL on to the plane of EVENT, of the ACTORS' PERFORMANCE.

I have already argued at length that in this work we dispense with FICTIONALITY (the play), since this requires as a *sine qua non* the ILLUSION of REPRESENTATION.

So we are left with nothing but REALITY.

There you have it!

The stage EVENT

is the REAL THING.

MADE NEW!

An invocation of recollection and

the past.

THE WORKING OF MEMORY.

Real because . . . gratuitous!

Post scriptum:

This is only the beginning where *Wielopole/Wielopole* is concerned.

It may well be that the longer it exists among us

the more readily it will yield up its well-kept secrets.